T0336598

TEACHING, TASKS, AND TRUST

TEACHING, TASKS, AND TRUST
FUNCTIONS OF THE PUBLIC EXECUTIVE

JOHN BREHM AND SCOTT GATES

A VOLUME IN THE RUSSELL SAGE FOUNDATION SERIES ON TRUST

Russell Sage Foundation • New York

The Russell Sage Foundation

The Russell Sage Foundation, one of the oldest of America's general purpose foundations, was established in 1907 by Mrs. Margaret Olivia Sage for "the improvement of social and living conditions in the United States." The Foundation seeks to fulfill this mandate by fostering the development and dissemination of knowledge about the country's political, social, and economic problems. While the Foundation endeavors to assure the accuracy and objectivity of each book it publishes, the conclusions and interpretations in Russell Sage Foundation publications are those of the authors and not of the Foundation, its Trustees, or its staff. Publication by Russell Sage, therefore, does not imply Foundation endorsement.

Library of Congress Cataloging-in-Publication Data

Brehm, John, 1960-
   Teaching, tasks, and trust : functions of the public executive / John Brehm and Scott Gates.
      p. cm.
   Includes bibliographical references and index.
   ISBN 978-0-87154-066-9
   1. Government executives. 2. Civil service—Personnel management. 3. Supervision of employees. I. Gates, Scott. II. Title.
   JF1601.B74 2008
   352.3—dc22

                                                                          2007044179

The paper used in this publication meets the minimum requirements of American National Standard for Information Sciences—Permanence of Paper for Printed Library Materials. ANSI Z39.48-1992.

Text design by Suzanne Nichols.

RUSSELL SAGE FOUNDATION
112 East 64th Street, New York, New York 10021
10 9 8 7 6 5 4 3 2 1

The Russell Sage Foundation Series on Trust

THE RUSSELL Sage Foundation Series on Trust examines the conceptual structure and the empirical basis of claims concerning the role of trust and trustworthiness in establishing and maintaining cooperative behavior in a wide variety of social, economic, and political contexts. The focus is on concepts, methods, and findings that will enrich social science and inform public policy.

The books in the series raise questions about how trust can be distinguished from other means of promoting cooperation and explore those analytic and empirical issues that advance our comprehension of the roles and limits of trust in social, political, and economic life. Because trust is at the core of understandings of social order from varied disciplinary perspectives, the series offers the best work of scholars from diverse backgrounds and, through the edited volumes, encourages engagement across disciplines and orientations. The goal of the series is to improve the current state of trust research by providing a clear theoretical account of the causal role of trust within given institutional, organizational, and interpersonal situations, developing sound measures of trust to test theoretical claims within relevant settings, and establishing some common ground among concerned scholars and policymakers.

Karen S. Cook
Russell Hardin
Margaret Levi

SERIES EDITORS

Previous Volumes in the Series

Contents

About the Authors

John Brehm is professor of political science at the University of Chicago.

Scott Gates is director of the Centre for the Study of Civil War, PRIO, and professor of political science at the Norwegian University of Science and Technology (NTNU).

John thanks his wife Kate and children Robin, Laurel, Joseph, and Jefferson.

Scott thanks his wife Ingeborg and children Christine, Alexandra, and Caroline.

Introduction

OUR FIRST book, *Working, Shirking, and Sabotage*, asked who, or what, controls the policy choices of bureaucrats. The overwhelming evidence indicated that individual bureaucrats' preferences had the greatest effect. Fellow bureaucrats, the public whom the bureaucrat serves, and supervisors played a role, but not the dominant role. Bureaucrats controlled their own behavior.

To understand behavior, we must get a sense of what motivates people. As for the underlying motivation of bureaucrats, we argued in *Working, Shirking, and Sabotage* that in addition to the material rewards (which are the major focus of economic and rational choice theories of organization), two categories of nonpecuniary rewards matter a great deal: functional and solidary rewards. Functional rewards are those one earns by virtue of accomplishment of the tasks of the job itself: a sense of satisfaction or achievement, the capacity for influencing the outcome of decisions, a belief that one is doing the right thing. Solidary rewards are those one earns by virtue of the social environment in which most bureaucrats work: how much do our peers, coworkers, people around us notice that we put in the extra effort? This does not mean that bureaucrats are solely motivated by nonpecuniary preferences. Just like the rest of us, material incentives matter a lot: a bump in base pay or an opportunity for an extended vacation are generally good things. What we emphasized, though, is that in an environment in which flexibility in the allocation of pecuniary rewards is severely constrained, as in a civil service, nonpecuniary rewards may matter even more.

Of course, there are other rewards that must matter, too. Some bureaucrats thrive because of the sense of power they have on the job. Other bureaucrats really do prize their longevity in the job—not a material incentive in a conventional sense, but if one thought about the long-run income potentials, that's one that should matter a lot.

Nonpecuniary preferences matter, and not only that they matter in observable ways, but by modes of association that may elude conventional modeling of bureaucracy. Assumptions that focus exclusively on rewards and punishments or the coercive aspects of supervision, miss

1

much that actually motivates. Too much emphasis has been placed on lazy good for nothing bureaucrats, who are only motivated through oversight, rewards, and punishment—many bureaucrats, in fact, work hard. This does not mean that no bureaucrat ever shirks. We have all suffered through interminable lines at various agencies staffed by thoroughly undermotivated bureaucrats on the other end. But in those agencies where bureaucrats do work hard, the most important explanations for how hard they work depend on the attributes of the bureaucrats, not of the nature of the supervision.

This does not mean that bureaucrats are saints and supervisors are superfluous impediments, but it does raise quite a big question (if not a problem) not addressed in *Working, Shirking, and Sabotage*: "Why do we have supervisors in the first place, if what matters are the attributes of the subordinates?" A truly inadequate answer might point to the aspects of selection into the bureaucratic environment, but that sounds like a part-time job to us. Another might be to suggest that supervisors matter because they are a (somewhat hollow) threat, but that one reels against what we argued before.

Long ago, Chester Barnard argued in *The Functions of the Executive* that all organizations, even private sector firms, are essentially cooperative. He went much further than we ever did by describing the coercive power of an executive to be a fiction. Moreover, Barnard contended that supervisors serve a combination of potential functions: "They are first to provide the system of communication; to promote the securing of essential efforts; and, third, to formulate and define purpose" (1938/1968, 217).

We turn to Barnard's multifaceted supervisor, serving a variety of roles, to help us address the problem for this book: "Why do we have supervisors in public bureaucracies?" This question and critique of *Working, Shirking, and Sabotage* raised by real bureaucrats and real supervisors, is the one that stings us the most. Our methods here will be similar to those of the first book: look to what the frontline bureaucrats say about the performance of their supervisors. We won't be looking, as many in our field prefer to do, at the putative successes of agency chiefs or bureau heads. In fact, most of our study will be about that most benighted of levels in an organizational chart, middle management.

But we will be much more particular: our focus will be on the assessments of lower level bureaucrats of their immediate supervisor's performance. Much of our data will be survey based, and we will do our best to attend to the plausible weaknesses of this mode. We also rely heavily on data that are observational, recording the actual performance of the subordinate bureaucrats.

We have quite a number of people to thank for their advice on this project. We are grateful, and they are blameless: Frank Baumgartner, Bill Bianco, Dan Carpenter, Brandice Canes-Wrone, Gretchen Casper, Cary

Coglianese, Doug Dion, Jeff Gill, Brad Gomez, Sandy Gordon, Jim Granato, Tom Hammond, Michael Heaney, Jeff Hill, Greg Huber, Brian Humes, Nils Haavardsson, Bryan Jones, Mark Jones, Jonathan Katz, Steven Kelman, Gary King, George Krause, Doowan Lee, Margaret Levy, Ola Listhaug, Skip Lupia, David Lowery, Bob Lowry, Monique Lyle, Jennifer Merolla, Nolan McCarty, Ken Meier, Roger Myerson, Gary Miller, Janet Owens, Jason Reifler, Per Morton Schliefloe, Carol and Bill Weissert, Ken Williams, and B. Dan Wood. We also wish to thank the Russell Sage Foundation for their support of a small research grant that facilitated our survey of the 2000 North Carolina Social Workers. We wish to thank the ICPSR for their public release of several data sets—the 1977 Police Services Study and the 1998 to 2000 Surveys of Federal Employees. We also wish to thank the Research Council of Norway for their financial support of this research. Any faults in our analysis are ours alone.

Chapter 4 is a revised version of the chapter we co-authored with Brad Gomez, "Donut Shops, Speed Traps, and Paperwork," which first appeared in George Krause and Kenneth Meier's *Politics, Policy, and Organizations: Frontiers in the Scientific Study of Bureaucracy* (2003).

Now, let's turn to the stinging question of why public bureaucracies use supervisors.

Chapter 1

Alternative Roles

S UPPOSE THAT it is your responsibility to encourage more effort from an employee on a task. The task might be straightforward (say, processing tax returns or collecting mail) or more complex (say, teaching children or managing the drug rehabilitation of recalcitrant clients). Even ascertaining how much effort your employee commits may be tricky. But let's shelve those issues for the moment and ask, how do I persuade my employee to work harder?

One solution—an intuitively natural one—is to monitor the employee's performance by some objective set of standards and to reward the employee for meeting the standards. This is both an old and a strikingly modern approach to the problem. The approach has roots which extend into the very beginnings of management science—the so-called scientific management approaches of Frederick Taylor, Henri Fayol, Luther Gulick, and others. More modern branches carry the fruit of serious game theoretic approaches to the management of the firm—the approach the disciplines of political science and economics call principal-agent theory, exemplified by Bengt Holmström (1979, 1982a) and Arrow (1985).[1] But though the approach is intuitive, it is probably inadequate advice to offer to the supervisor. We will refer to these approaches as coercive, those that emphasize monitoring performance and rewarding for meeting standards (and possibly punishing for not doing so).

Instead, we may need to reach into other aspects of the theory of organizations and of management and look for alternative advice for the supervisor. The enterprise of this book is to identify what three of these roles may offer in the way of advice: training, brokering of trust, and task management. None of these roles are especially new, all date to one or another aspect of organization theory and management science. Nor are they exclusive and exhaustive, and perhaps not even entirely independent of the coercive aspects of supervision.[2] We argue, though, that they

4

are intimately connected, and that the connection stems from the problem of organizational ambiguity.

Ambiguity is a touchstone reference for organization theorists, differing in important ways from its more familiar cousin, uncertainty. Both ambiguity and uncertainty denote states of unfamiliarity and unpredictability about outcomes. An uncertain state is one that can be resolved with additional information, whereas an ambiguous one remains unfamiliar and unpredictable even after information is acquired. An uncertain state of the world, for example, would be whether it will rain on a given day. At the end of that day, the answer is definitive. The corresponding state of the world is whether it would be good if it rained on a given day. For the farmer fearful of drought, a rainy day is unambiguously good; for the would-be picnicker, perhaps not.

This is a toy example, but it serves well to differentiate between uncertainty and ambiguity. At its most basic, ambiguity is about uncertainty of probability, and thereby serves to distinguish risk from ambiguity (Knight 1921). This is what Daniel Ellsberg shows in his thought experiment that people prefer to bet on events they know more about (1961). This is Ellsberg's paradox. Indeed, there is an aversion to ambiguity. In this guise, ambiguity is related to issues of subjective expected utility, common knowledge of rationality, and consistent alignment of beliefs (for more on subjective expected utility theory, see Camerer and Weber 1992; for a discussion about common knowledge of rationality and consistent alignment of beliefs, see Hargreaves-Heap and Varoufakis 1995). But our conceptualization of ambiguity is deeper, as our example regarding rain demonstrates. For our purposes, ambiguity is more than uncertainty about the probability of an event. It is about ambiguity over the utility of different outcomes.

The problem of ambiguity is pointed for public bureaucracies. At root, the problem of ambiguity for a public bureaucracy rises from the contradictory tasks that we, the citizens, expect bureaucracies to achieve (for the original advancement of this argument, see Wilson 1967). Bureaucracies must be equitable, and treat all inputs identically. After all, the very core idea of rational-legal authority is the idea of regularity and consistency in how the bureaucratic authority deals with the polity (Weber 1947; Finer 1941). But bureaucracies may also exercise considerable discretion, and do so because the polity believes that some cases are best handled as individuals and exceptions to rational-legal rule (Lipsky 1980).

Several other equally competing standards can be added to those of equitability and discretion. Contemporary polities prefer that their bureaucracies be honest institutions, not vehicles for the personal advancement of the bureaucrat, or, for that matter, for the advancement of privileged members of society. Likewise, an honorable goal for a bureaucracy is to be open to public scrutiny, to be more democratic in the rule of law than perhaps legislatures can be in the writing of law. But what if some sectors of a polity lack the political resources? In being fair, bureaucracies may have to cater to those without resources, to intrude politics into policy choices (Long 1949). And though it may rarely be the specific maximand of any particular bureaucrat, efficiency in the use of scarce resources may also be a bureaucratic standard (Niskanen 1975).

All of these dimensions—equitability, discretion, fairness, honesty, openness, efficiency—compete with one another, as much as they are all laudable goals. Further, it would be the height of arrogance to assert that some form of hierarchy exists among them: at times, all are candidates for the prime objective of a bureaucracy.

If these are the standards by which a bureaucrat must measure his or her performance, even one who is not self-maximizing (for wealth, perks, power, or leisure) is caught on the horns of ambiguity.

We see three basic questions confronting the subordinate in a bureaucracy:

- What are the bounds of what I can or cannot do?

- What should I do first? What is most important?

- What happens if I exercise discretion over either of these first two choices?

The first is not merely a question of aversion to sanctions or limits of authority. As the classic work by Daniel Katz and Robert Kahn laid out, *role ambiguity* was defined "as lack of information regarding supervisory evaluation of one's work, about opportunities for advancement, scope of responsibility, and expectations of role senders" (1978, 190). Elements of the problem of role ambiguity are as old as any concept in the social sciences—Émile Durkheim's idea of *anomie*, for example, is derived from a sense of normlessness in the allocation of rewards and opportunities (1893/1997). Consider one of our core examples in this volume: social workers are swamped with problems of role ambiguity, which stem from the contradictory expectations that the polity heaps on performance. Although we may have warm fuzzy images about social workers, and the nurturing aspects of their jobs (for example, extending welfare benefits, providing counseling), we also have highly punitive ones about other aspects of their work (for example, removing children from homes, assignment to mental health facilities).

In a recent book, Bryan Jones (2001) notes that ambiguity in public life can create situations in which not only the problems but also the potential solutions are ambiguous. This formulation extends from the famous work by Michael Cohen, James March, and Johan Olsen (1972) on the inflammatorily named garbage can model of organizational choice.

Jones's key elaboration is that knowing what to do may reference the tasks of advocacy of particular remedies, implementation of those remedies, or even identification of the problems.

In their article, James Breaugh and Joseph Colihan (1994) test the construct validity of the role ambiguity concept. Part of the difficulty with the concept is that it remains to be established whether role ambiguity is inherently noxious (see Kahn et al. 1964; Kagan 1972; Sorrentino and Short 1986), or is noxious because it interferes with functional performance (Sawyer 1992). Breaugh and Colihan identify three specific types of job ambiguity: employee uncertainty about the standards a supervisor uses to determine whether job performance is satisfactory (performance evaluation ambiguity), uncertainty about the methods or procedures one should use in work (work method ambiguity), and uncertainty about when to perform which tasks (temporal role ambiguity). Using confirmatory factor methods, Breaugh and Colihan establish that the three types of job ambiguity are indeed separable, correlated not only with one another, but strongly also with job satisfaction and satisfaction with the employer. Likewise, Linda King and Daniel King (1990) also see multiple facets to role ambiguity: what is required, how responsibilities are to be met, uncertainty about whose expectations must be met, and with what consequences. King and King are, however, much less sanguine than Breaugh and Colihan about the construct validity of the role ambiguity measures, and conclude that there is considerable ambiguity about role ambiguity.

On the other side—the effects of role ambiguity on job satisfaction compared with other potentially noxious qualities—there is equally strong evidence. John French and his colleagues (1982) argue that job strain results principally from a misfit between the workplace environment and the person's attributes, instead of responsibility or work. In a reestimation of the same data using more sophisticated confirmatory factor analytic techniques, Jeffrey Edwards and Van Harrison (1993) find that, although one can separate job strain into multiple dimensions (complexity, role ambiguity, responsibility for persons, and workload), only role ambiguity consistently provides a strong explanation for job dissatisfaction.

One possible mechanism for the noxiousness of role ambiguity is that it may heighten sensitivity to potential threats. In a study of the relationship between anxiety and ambiguity, Colin MacLeod and Ilan Cohen (1993) find, in a set of experiments on undergraduates, that anxious subjects in a state of role ambiguity are more likely to read text (and, presumptively, other messages) as threatening than those who are not anxious about role ambiguity. A second postulated mechanism (Webster and Kruglanski 1994) is that some subjects may have a greater need for cognitive closure about tasks, much as some people experience a greater need for cognition (Cacioppo and Petty 1982).

The second question—what should I do first? what is most important?—arises because few bureaucracies have the resources to accomplish all of the tasks within their purview. Prioritizing what has to be done when—and, as a necessary consequence, deciding what will not be done ever—is a fundamental ambiguity for bureaucrats. We devote several chapters to the problem of task allocation, which is one way to resolve task ambiguity.

The final question—what happens if I exercise discretion over either of these first two choices?—concerns political accountability. Where the Weberian ideal-type bureaucracy required clear lines of political accountability, few real bureaucracies feature single threaded lines of command. Returning to our social worker example, the subordinate social worker has a supervisor to whom he or she reports, but may also come into conflict with subordinates or supervisors in other divisions, with the director of social services, with local political officials, with reporters for the local media, and with citizens directly. The lines of political accountability become even more tangled when one accounts for the competing political interests of these many sources.[3]

Organizational ambiguity describes the conditions that arise in trying to answer the two fundamental questions every subordinate employee will have about the supervisor's expectations for performance:

- What do I do?

- What happens to me if I do it?

Organizations swim in ambiguity, and public organizations especially so.

We ask bureaucracies to do too many things, with too few resources, and where even those things may represent contradictory demands. Consider the public school math teacher. She is supposed to accomplish the core mission: to educate the pupils in a specific subject. She is probably underpaid, and probably severely so. She probably has too large a class. She may have a chalkboard. She is supposed to keep order in the classroom, which may be all the more difficult given the typically large class size. She should monitor the behavior of her students, she needs to attend to the needs of those who are having difficulty with their homework, needs to keep the attention of those who are working at the pace of the class, and even needs to keep the super-high achievers still motivated.

The problem is that we have little agreement on just what she is supposed to cover. As all of us who have been through public schools may (perhaps painfully) recall, a typical progression in math classes is from basic skills, through algebra, analytic geometry, advanced algebra, trigonometry, pre-calculus, calculus, and perhaps beyond. But some schools may, perhaps rightfully, argue that our teacher needs to cover calculus just before college, and insert another topic (discrete math and statistics are common). Other schools (and parents) may expect teachers to combine some of these topics. Still others may prefer calculus to come earlier in the academic sequence. The question of the best way to teach is ambiguous because it does not have a definitive solution.

That said, it does not stop us from imposing at least some standards on performance—that of the pupils, the teachers, and the schools. The No Child Left Behind Act calls for mandatory end-of-year testing of children's performance in public schools, ostensibly to permit students to relocate away from failing schools. Similar policies are common in the states. This is an exemplar of the coercive approach to public management: insist on the output of the public school (and, more directly, the teacher) be measured by some objective set of standards, and punish (by permitting the students to relocate to other schools) schools that do not achieve.

A funny thing happens. Schools, and teachers, are quite familiar with the year-end tests and the consequences of inadequate performance. The teachers may explicitly adopt a policy of teaching to the test, that is, where the sole focus of the year's instruction is the test itself. Similar policies may emerge in the nation's AP exams. This is one answer to the problem of measuring performance and an instantiation of achievement.

It is not, however, necessarily the right answer. What about those problem students, who are found in every school in the country? When the end-of-year tests come around, teachers may choose to "cheat" on them by encouraging slow learners and distracting students from attending school that day. Some students may have learning difficulties, such as attention deficit disorder, dyslexia, or dysgraphia. How much should we adjust the test, either in scoring it or in how students take it, to accommodate such students? Is teaching to test an appropriate way to encourage more ambiguous forms of learning, such as fostering a love of learning itself?

Public bureaucracies face exceptional ambiguity, in that supervisors and employees must make choices about unattainable goals that often contradict each other and for which we underequip them.

Our first book on performance in public bureaucracies, *Working, Shirking, and Sabotage* (Brehm and Gates 1997), claimed that to understand which bureaucrats put positive, zero, or negative effort at their jobs, one should really look more to the bureaucrats than to their supervisors. And so, as many readers have commented, this raises the question as to why we even have supervisors. A justly appropriate question, but not one we originally considered. Our purpose in this volume is to suggest that supervisors do meet very functional, very desirable purposes within public organizations, just not those that fall squarely within coercive conceptions of the organization.

We will retain our dyadic approach to thinking about supervision. Our focus will be on individual bureaucrats, but in thinking about the alternative conceptions of the supervisor. We believe that such an inside the box examination is vastly superior to the highly aggregated approach.

In the remainder of this chapter, we first provide an outline of the ancien régime, the coercive approach. One should, after all, really understand what one is rejecting before rejecting it. We then review the three alternative approaches to management—training, trust brokering, and task management—and explain some alternative (and why we choose not to cover them here). Finally, we outline the broader plan of the book.

The Coercive Approach

Principal-agent models focus on an individual (the principal) who contracts work from an agent. The agent's motivations and ability (or type) may be unknown, as may be his or her effort on the job. The former— unknown type—is classified as a problem of *adverse selection.* The term comes from the insurance literature, and we credit Kenneth Arrow (1985) for articulating it. The latter problem—unknown action—is one of *moral hazard,* another term from the insurance literature.

In the insurance industry, one problem for the company will be that some individuals may buy insurance only because they expect to make a claim. The desperately ill patient is a classic example. This is adverse selection.

In an organizational setting, adverse selection refers to a supervisor's inability to gauge the subordinate's preferences and abilities. How might the principal resolve this problem? Perhaps by verifying the agent's type through intensive interviews in screening candidates, or by probationary periods for hires, or by expectations of certain qualifications for the job, similar to the mandatory blood tests before securing life insurance.

The moral hazard problem also affects the insurance industry. Here, instead of purchasing insurance because one expects to need it, the purchaser changes his or her behavior. In an organizational setting, the action of subordinates focuses on degree of effort (or propensity for shirking) and latent opportunism. How can one resolve the problem? One might monitor the subordinate's behavior, or change the incentive structure (by increasing penalties for bad behavior or increasing rewards for good behavior), or even the entire system in favor of incentive-compatible regulations, just as the insurance company might reduce rates for drivers with good records or dispense rewards for those who can prove they do not smoke.

Sometimes the problem may be particularly pointed, as when there is a team production condition (Alchian and Demsetz 1972), where all the principal sees is the total output from a team of agents. At this, the incentive to free ride on the contributions of others becomes an additionally strong component of the moral hazard problem. Bengt Holmström (1982a) extends this analysis by demonstrating that there is no budget-balancing revenue-sharing scheme that can effectively induce all members of a team to work and for none to shirk. In other words, ultimately, a principal is stuck with the moral hazard problem.

The intuitive way to rectify both the adverse selection and moral hazard problems might be to improve the selection of employees, monitor their output on the job, and pay them according to that output on the job. An early advocate of scientific management, Frederick Taylor, argued for just that approach, which was grounded in four principles: accumulating all the knowledge about the job, scientifically selecting the workman, offer incentives for good performance, and reconsidering the division of work itself (see Taylor 1911). These themes of coercion appear again toward the end of the twentieth century in work related to organizational oversight in the public sector (see, for example, McCubbins and Schwartz 1984; Fiorina 1986; McCubbins, Noll, and Weingast 1989). Roderick Kiewiet and Mathew McCubbins feature a set of coercive powers available to supervisors: hiring and firing, design of compensation (contracts), monitoring and institutional checks (1991). These have a broad intuitive appeal.

Indeed, the approach is intuitive, but it is also incomplete. Chester Barnard, an executive at New Jersey Bell Telephone, suggested that organizations function more as cooperative ventures rather than coercive ones. Indeed, he wrote of the "fiction of the superior authority" (1938/1968, 166). Although his book, *Functions of the Executive,* serves as something of a model for this volume, Barnard is too harsh in his assessment of the fiction of coercive authority. Coercive authority can work: people do lose their jobs due to underperformance, are paid piece-rate, and are selected after careful evaluations of their capacities. We argue, however, that such coercive roles, as emphasized first by Taylor and later by scholars of the economics of the firm, are misplaced in studies of public bureaucracy.

The coercive model has limited applicability to private sector firms, but even more profound ones in regard to public sector organizations. First, public institutions are not governed by the laws of supply and demand. Except in cases where they compete to provide services, bureaucracies tend to operate as monopolies prone to oversupply policy output. There are revenues and budgets, but no profits (and with implications for principal-agent models, no residuals). Such limitations call into question whether principal-agent models apply to the public sector. Second, civil service laws significantly constrain public sector executives from using coercion in any form. A supervisor has, unlike his or her private sector counterparts, limited ability to redistribute pecuniary rewards to reward or sanction subordinates. Moreover, the ultimate enforcement—firing someone—is extraordinarily difficult and typically possible only in cases of gross negligence or misconduct. Third, bureaucratic policy output is notoriously difficult to monitor. Public sector policy output typically does not lend itself to piece-rate production. Ultimately, public sector organizations are inherently infused with ambiguity. There is almost never a bottom line, but rather many overlapping and competing goals. All organizations, even small private sector firms, face problems of ambiguity, but public sector organizations must overcome more fundamental issues of ambiguity—ambiguities in terms of goals, design, and organization. Clearly, the coercive role of a public sector manager is even more limited than that of a supervisor in the private sector. What then, are the functions of the public executive?

Alternative Functions

Let us look at three alternatives to the coercive roles of management: training, cultivating trust, and task management.

By training, we mean two distinct things. One is the cultivation of prosocial preferences: to learn to want to do what the principal wants. This quite possibly happens in some organizations, though the record is rather mixed. Another meaning is the clarification of the boundaries of acceptable and unacceptable behavior. Every organization has rules, whether formally denoted or not. As Charles Perrow (1986) argues, organizations without formal rules require a fair amount of exploration by the organization members, and usually entail some significant pain to discover. We explore both aspects of training.

By cultivating trust, we mean one thing: to what extent does the supervisor gain the trust of his or her subordinates, and by what mechanism? The fuzzy part of the argument might be with the mechanism. Sometimes, subordinates express trust in their supervisor because of a belief about his or her intentions, or one about the supervisor's character or capacities. We argue that supervisors can gain the trust of their subordinates by providing cover for them: acting as interference to prevent others from interacting directly with the subordinate (such as members of the media, other supervisors, or other political superordinates). This is a specific trust owing to a specific content.

By task management, we refer to the capacities that supervisors may have at their disposal to persuade subordinates to work on some subset of tasks at the omission of effort on others. The supervisor may prefer that the subordinate allocate effort on tasks A and B instead of tasks C and D, whereas the subordinate may prefer to work on tasks B and D. In this scenario, the supervisor's leverage is of effort at B.

We believe that a full understanding of just what we mean by training, trust brokering, and task management, an overview of the chapters to follow is warranted. But, first, let us give a preliminary sketch of the idea that motivates our interest in these specific functions, as well as why we believe they are intimately related.

Sometimes, taking a job in the public sector entails the possibility that a great number of people and institutions will be watching what you do and how well you do it. Sometimes the rules for what you can and cannot do are explicit, but other times they require clarification. Sometimes they contradict one another. How does one respond?

One response, if you can get away with it, might be do to as little as possible. This is what we refer to as shirking, or leisure-shirking (Brehm and Gates 1997). But another response, especially for public sector employees motivated by functional preferences, would be to contribute to the purposes of the organization, perhaps even beyond how the organization tangibly rewards you. Let's call this working. There is also a third, less commonly observed response, which would be to consciously undermine those rules through diligent efforts, which we have referred to as sabotage (Brehm and Gates 1997).

How do you know which rules (formal or informal) are the most important to follow and when? The first function of the public supervisor that we explore is the role of training, understood here as the clarification of boundaries. Of course, other parties, such as one's co-workers, may be even more important in clarifying the rules. If the supervisor takes the lead role in training the subordinates, then folk cultures may be more under control and the norms for working instead of shirking can take charge.

There is a flip side to the supervisor taking such a strong role in training her subordinates: she has to stand up for them against all other parties who may be interested in their behavior. Other supervisors may put demands for diversions of the subordinate's time or just disagree with how this particular supervisor sets her priorities for performance. The local media hardly ever report about the successes of bureaucracies, most of which are routine and mundane and ordinary. But bureaucratic failures illustrate the alleged heartlessness, cruelty, and arbitrariness of those bureaucracies and make for great headlines. Local government officials may also become interested before or after such coverage. There are many people and entities out there who can make your performance a cause for personal grief.

We call this second role trust brokering. Supervisors who stand up for their employees by providing political cover against those other interested parties earn their employees' trust. This is hard work and may be even politically costly for the supervisor. But brokering trust earns something, namely, that those subordinates who feel they have the discretion to do what is right, do it, and have the full faith and confidence of their supervisor, and accord their supervisor leeway.

Leeway is essential. As we have written and will further explain in this volume, bureaucracies generally do many different things. Of course, some perform a highly circumscribed set of tasks, such as the Social Security Administration or the U.S. Postal Service. James Wilson referred to these as production agencies (1989). Most bureaucracies have more to do than time to do it.

Supervisors must therefore choose among these tasks, setting priorities, perhaps encouraging subordinates to perform less interesting or even onerous or unpleasant tasks. Given the limited flexibility of the public sector, compared to the private sector, such allocations are extremely important for the public executive. This third function is task management.

The rough summary of our argument is this: because of the fundamental background of ambiguity behind public bureaucracies, there is a key function that supervisors must perform in training their subordinates about what is allowed and what is not; in exchange, the subordinates only trust their supervisors when that supervisor shields the subordinates from intrusions by others; in doing so, the supervisor gains more leeway to assign tasks.

Plan of the Book

We develop this argument by taking several small steps, applying a mix of methods, models, and data.

Chapter 2 looks to empirical data on the effectiveness of training in real bureaucracies, here, drawing on our own data on social workers in North Carolina and three waves of extensive surveys of employees in the federal bureaucracy.

Chapter 3 explores the likely futility of training as a cultivation of pro-social preferences. Our tool is a computational model that closely parallels the structure of a basic principal-agency relationship.

In chapter 4, we develop a cooperative game theoretic model of the task allocation problem. We prove the existence of a cooperative solution, called a core, within a budget that depends solely on exchanges of perks for tasks.

In chapter 5, we analyze the task allocation problem in practice, in a study of task allocation within the police forces of three separate cities.

In chapter 6, we articulate a very simple (noncooperative) game theoretic model of trust, based on an extension of the trust-honor game by David Kreps (1990), and again explicating this model in the context of the social worker data.

In chapter 7, we explore the same problem—that of the cultivation of trust—by examining the behavior of federal bureaucrats.

Chapter 8 unifies the three functions and argues that the unique problems of ambiguity for subordinates in public bureaucracies create conditions under which training clarifies boundaries, trust results from supervisors standing up for subordinates, and trusted supervisors have greater latitude in assigning tasks. We conclude with speculation about the generalizability of our findings to the broader problems of leadership within organization, and the organization's performance as an aggregate.

This volume draws on three sources of data from different types of bureaucracies: three surveys of federal government workers conducted by the Office of Personnel Management (OPM) in 1998, 1999, and 2000; participant observation data on police officers (Ostrom, Parks, and Whittaker 1982); and our own surveys of social workers in North Carolina. We use three different theoretical modeling techniques: simulations or agent-based modeling; noncooperative games; and a cooperative game. We also draw on a variety of statistical models, including first principal component scale construction, mixture models, and three-stage least squares.

PART I

TRAINING

Chapter 2

Empirical Data on Training

WHAT IS the strength of the evidence that training clarifies the boundaries between appropriate and inappropriate behavior, or between what is meritorious and what leads to punishment? Training is one way to make the bureaucrat's job less ambiguous, not so much by the addition of information as a way to reduce uncertainty, but by enacting (Weick 1979) a path out of the ambiguity. Enacting, to use Karl Weick's phrase, entails "the important role that people play in creating the environments that impose on them" (5).

Consider the delightful distinction between enacting and informing that opens Weick's book, itself an excerpt from Simons (1976, 29). Three umpires are discussing how they call pitches in the game:

> The story goes that three umpires disagreed about the task of calling balls and strikes. The first one said, "I calls them as they is." The second one said, "I calls them as I sees them." The third and cleverest umpire said, "They ain't nothin' till I calls them."

As any baseball fan would readily attest, there is a difference between the pitch that the umpire calls a strike (but appears to be outside the strike zone) and one that is plainly over the plate. The umpire does not inform the game, in the sense that that umpire has definitively determined the fairness of his call; the umpire has, however, enacted a pathway by which the game will proceed.

The ambiguity the bureaucratic supervisor confronts with his or her subordinates stems from two basic questions subordinates pose: What do I do now? What will happen to me if I do it? As we discussed in chapter 1, the answers to both are multifold and possibly contradictory: take care of your paperwork, or put the paperwork aside, you need to follow up on this case; we can let that case slide, or this case really matters to the higher-ups. Supervisors may not reduce the ambiguity, but they can enact the subordinates' and supervisor's way out of the condition.

How does training materialize in terms of effort by the employees? We had already established that one form of training meant very little for overall productivity, in the form where the supervisor diverts some of the stream of residuals to induce pro-social preferences on the part of the subordinates. To be sure, the subordinates became happier, but productivity did not increase. But what about the alternative form of training as a way of clarifying the boundary between acceptable and unacceptable behavior?

One advantage of this approach—training as boundary clarifier—is that it is more closely wed to the problems of ambiguity that premise this book. If organizational processes and outputs were transparent, there would be little need to clarify boundaries. Most bureaucracies, however, are in the business of working through ambiguities at the level of inputs, outputs, or outcomes. Policy inputs denote the raw materials the bureaucracy transforms. In the case of the school teacher, the policy inputs include not only the schoolchildren, but also the textbooks, projects, and classrooms, even peer students or peer teachers. Policy inputs for forest rangers in the 1940s and 1950s referred to lumber, grazing area, and mines, and now must include management of resources far beyond that scope, such as interdiction of narcotics traffic. Although the particular identity of the input may be unambiguous, its relevance for the bureaucratic process is much more in doubt. Sometimes the policy outputs may be unambiguous: the Social Security Administration cuts checks for retirees of a congressionally mandated amount. But sometimes policy outputs may be more obscure, whether because the agent performs his or her task out of sight of the principal, as in the Forest Service, or because the agent prefers that his or her actions not be observable, as perhaps among wage and hour employees at the Department of Labor (Wilson 1989, 165). Moreover, policy outcomes may be obscure: outcomes are the result, presumably, of the outputs of the agency. The police forces of every major city conduct regular patrols, which are somewhat observable, but the underlying question must be to what extent the patrols reduce crime, which is the desirable output.

Under such conditions, there may not be a right way to transform an input into an output in pursuit of an outcome. There may be many right ways, there may be no known right way, or there may just be rampant confusion about the process. What training as a boundary-clarifier does is to permit the supervisor the authority to declare what is acceptable and what is unacceptable on the part of the actions of the subordinate. To the extent that such clarification reduces friction between the subordinate and supervisor, that is all probably to the good. But further, to the extent that there is broader social agreement about the virtues of staying inside the boundaries, then that is at least initial evidence about the effect of training in cultivating pro-social preferences of the first kind.

An alternative approach is a search for empirical evidence regarding the effectiveness of training. We will stipulate that though it is conceivable that one could obtain and demonstrate evidence about the cultivation of pro-social preferences (or perhaps organizational socialization), but there are numerous research barriers. For one, given that the object would be to examine change in preferences, the ideal data would follow particular individuals over time. For another, there are such strong social desirability effects at work that honest measurement is a dubious prospect: who would admit to preferences that diverge from the pro-social preferences, when asked?

For entirely different reasons (as we will explicate in chapter 3), we are skeptical about the long-run utility of this particular view of training. It is possible to train subordinates to become happier with their lot (under some very binding constraints), but our evidence is that they are no more productive. Moreover, the binding constraints really do pinch: subordinates have to prefer the task at the outset, and a positive response has to be available.

Thus the second advantage of boundary clarification as an alternative approach is that it is probably much more measurable than the cultivation of pro-social preferences. Indeed, the federal government has spent millions of dollars over the last decade to try to evaluate the effectiveness of one experiment in boundary clarification, the so-called Reinvention of Government. The program, begun and concluded under the Clinton administration, provided for streamlining of inputs as well as for a more concerted effort to measure the attitudes and activities of the subordinates themselves. The Bush administration continued with similar initiatives, though characteristically not closely identified with Clinton or Gore initiatives. Although measurement should not drive away desirable research of other approaches, it is foolish to turn away from data that is already at hand.

As the reader will imminently see, we have the advantage of three separate bases of data: federal employees, social workers in North Carolina, and police officers in three American cities in the 1970s. We have identified aspects of the federal employee and social worker data that are on point for the present question. The third data set examines police officers, but it is not suitable for the present analysis. We introduce this data collection in chapter 5.

Federal Employees

The Office of Personnel Management conducted three surveys between 1998 and 2000 as part of Vice President Gore's initiative on reinventing government, dubbed the National Partnership for Reinventing

Government surveys. This initiative aimed to make the federal bureaucracy more flexible and more responsive to citizen demands by such activities as setting performance goals and clarifying standards for good performance. OPM conducted the first of these studies in August 1998. Surveys were distributed to 34,401 employees in forty-eight agencies, randomly selected in a stratified design, of which 13,657 were returned (for a response rate of 40 percent). OPM administered the second in September 1999, distributing the surveys to 32,265 employees in the same agencies, of which 12,755 were returned, again for a 40 percent response rate. The final survey, the 2000 wave, was distributed to a sample of 50,844 federal employees, of which 21,157 were returned, for a response rate of 42 percent. These are obviously very large surveys yielding a sampling error of only 2 percent.

Training

The four questions asked in all three waves are a useful point of comparison across the agencies:

- Does the manager communicate the organization's mission, vision, and values? *(Manager communicates).*

- Has your immediate supervisor organized your work group effectively to get the work done? *(Supervisor organized).*

- Do employees receive training and guidance in providing high quality customer service? *(Employees trained).*

- Do employees receive the training they need to perform their jobs, for example, on-the-job training, conferences, workshops? *(Receive needed training).*

These questions, and the tables that present the answers to them, demonstrate how static the federal employees' evaluations of their environment are.

If one were to put these questions up against a standard administration theory text, we suspect that there would be points of overlap and omission. The first question, *Manager communicates,* speaks more to the question of whether the frontline supervisor is able to cultivate a sense of the organizational mission and the general purpose of the organization. Nonetheless, that kind of communication is essential to the general issue of reducing the ambiguity of the organization.

The second question, *Supervisor organized,* omits quite a lot of the nitty gritty mechanisms that the supervisor might need to employ to bring the work group together, yet it is still directed essentially at the question of subordinate performance.

Table 2.1   Distribution of Sense of Training, Office of
Personnel Management

		SD	D	N	A	SA
Manager communicates	1998	9.5	18.4	15.8	43.4	12.9
	1999	11.1	19.2	16.5	41.4	11.9
	2000	10.1	17.8	19.4	41.3	11.4
Supervisor organized	1998	11.6	17.8	15.7	36.8	18.0
	1999	12.4	16.6	17.3	37.8	16.0
	2000	10.8	14.2	18.0	39.5	17.5
Employees trained	1998	11.3	24.1	24.4	33.6	6.7
	1999	12.5	25.6	24.3	31.4	6.2
	2000	11.6	22.5	25.4	33.0	7.5
Receive needed training	1998	9.4	19.2	16.6	44.1	10.7
	1999	10.8	19.7	15.9	42.6	11.0
	2000	9.5	18.1	14.6	43.5	14.2

Source: Authors' compilation from 1998 to 2000 National Partnership for Reinventing Government Employee Surveys.
Note: Cell entries are the percentage either "strongly disagreeing" (SD), "disagreeing" (D), "neither agreeing nor disagreeing" (N), "agreeing" (A) or "strongly agreeing" (SA) with the question. Sample sizes were 13,689 in 1998, 18,154 in 1999, and 31,975 in 2000. All surveys were probability samples drawn to represent the universe of federal employees.

The third question, *Employees trained,* we see as largely unobjectionable; yet there is still an important point of comment in the reference to customer service. As with the social workers later in this volume and in our original study, bureaucrats adopt a for-service outlook that is reflected in the use of the word *customer.*

The fourth question, *Receive training,* suggests a slew of possible means by which the bureaucrats could become trained. These are, by nature of the question, left to the imagination of the respondent to complete, but we think that the question is sufficiently suggestive.

Table 2.1 presents the marginals for the National Partnership for Reinventing Government employee surveys. What we find especially striking about this table is just how flat it is: with very few exceptions, the cells change by only a percent or two from year to year, and not really in a predictable pattern. In three categories, the percentages change by 3.5 or 3.6 percent. Most notable of the three exceptions is the percentage that reports strongly agreeing that they receive the needed training, which jumps from 10.70 to 14.20 percent from 1999 to 2000.[1] One should be extremely cautious about drawing any interpretations of meaning from this and the other changes, given that sampling error would yield a statistically significant result in one in twenty samples.

In all, one would conclude from these marginals that the supervisors do a good job of communicating the agency mission, that they appear to be generally well organized, and that the agency as a whole does a good job of making sure that subordinates receive appropriate on-the-job training. Of the four questions, the one that respondents rate the agencies to be underperforming—and this not by much—is that respondents feel that they are not as well trained for the job as outsiders expect them to be.

On an agency-by-agency basis (see figure 2.1), there are some more instructive results. First, we compute the loadings for each scale using confirmatory factor analysis. We therefore must specify the logical structure of the factors and their indicators in advance. Our goal in this case is to find roughly equivalent factor loadings, and with the exception of three indicators, that is exactly what we obtain. The full factor loadings (for all three scales used in this chapter) may be found in table 2.8.

Next, we display the computed scores from this confirmatory factor model using a dotplot. Dotplots were invented by William Cleveland (1985) as a quick way to compare scores across a large number of categories. The categories are the agencies responding to the Reinventing Government surveys. The axis represents the range (on a fixed scale) that the particular variable might take, such that the variable records the average of the first principal component (roughly speaking, a kind of weighted averaging). We use the main digit to indicate the score: that is, 8 denotes results for 1998, 9 for 1999, and 0 for 2000. We sort the agencies by department, except for a few cabinet agencies, which we list at the bottom.

The general picture from the first dotplot is one of consistency, but, of course, not all agencies are the same. Employees at the National Air and Space Administration (NASA) have a very high opinion of the level of training, and consistently so. These respondents express this support for three out of the four questions beyond a statistically significant degree: *Manager communicates, Supervisor organized*, and *Receive needed training*. Considering the extraordinary complexity of the NASA career path, perhaps it is not in the least surprising to find evidence of such a positive attitude toward training by the supervisors.

Respondents from several agencies report unusually low levels of training. As seen in figure 2.1, respondents from the Federal Aviation Authority (FAA), Occupational Safety and Health (OSHA), Immigration and Naturalization Service (INS), and the Health Care Financing Administration (HCFA) report less training and on-the-job training than respondents from other agencies.

With regard to other aspects of training, respondents affiliated with the Federal Emergency Management Agency (FEMA) and Food Safety consistently state that manager communication is not as strong as it is at other agencies. Social Security respondents report that their supervisors are not as organized as those at other agencies.

Figure 2.1   Respondents' Report of Training

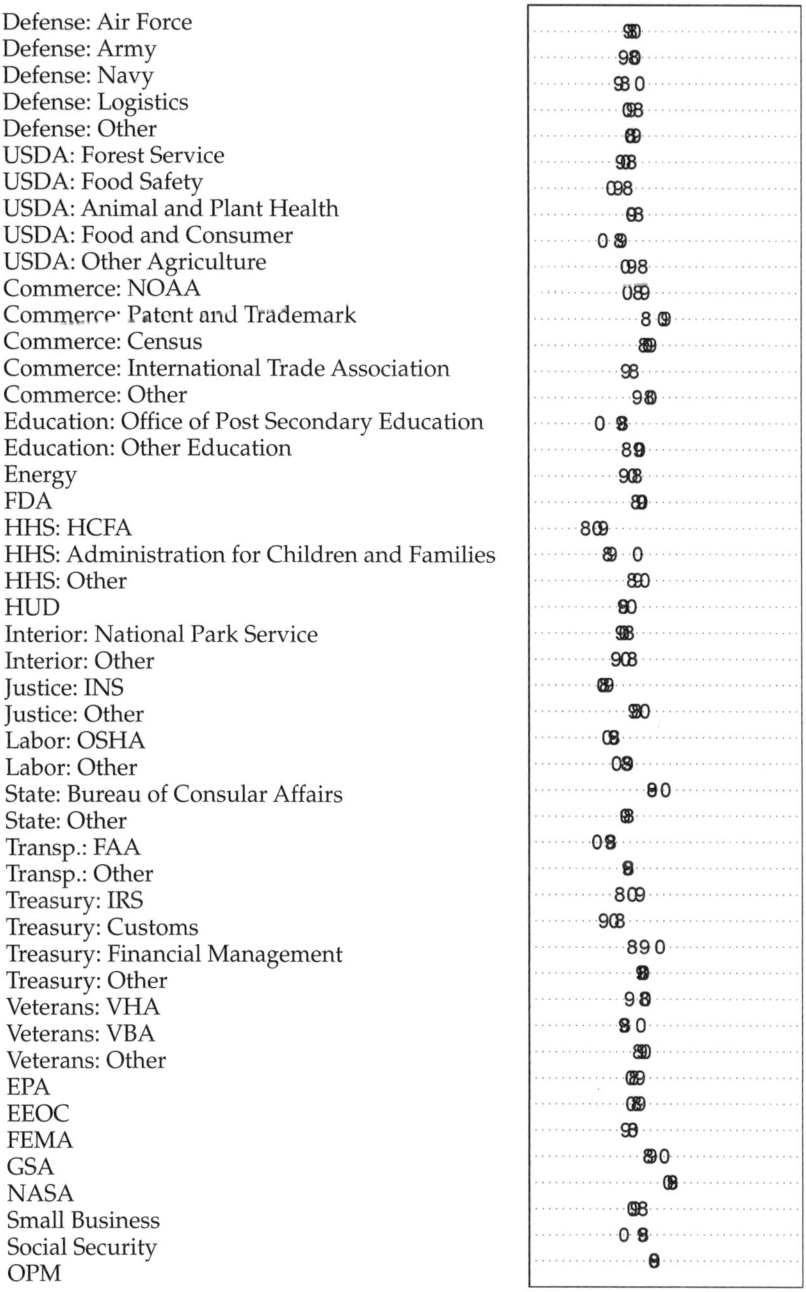

Defense: Air Force
Defense: Army
Defense: Navy
Defense: Logistics
Defense: Other
USDA: Forest Service
USDA: Food Safety
USDA: Animal and Plant Health
USDA: Food and Consumer
USDA: Other Agriculture
Commerce: NOAA
Commerce: Patent and Trademark
Commerce: Census
Commerce: International Trade Association
Commerce: Other
Education: Office of Post Secondary Education
Education: Other Education
Energy
FDA
HHS: HCFA
HHS: Administration for Children and Families
HHS: Other
HUD
Interior: National Park Service
Interior: Other
Justice: INS
Justice: Other
Labor: OSHA
Labor: Other
State: Bureau of Consular Affairs
State: Other
Transp.: FAA
Transp.: Other
Treasury: IRS
Treasury: Customs
Treasury: Financial Management
Treasury: Other
Veterans: VHA
Veterans: VBA
Veterans: Other
EPA
EEOC
FEMA
GSA
NASA
Small Business
Social Security
OPM

Source: Authors' compilation from 1998 to 2000 National Partnership for Reinventing Government Employee Surveys, Office of Personnel Management.

Overall training is remarkably consistent from year to year. Whether a much longer-term study would turn up equivalent results is, naturally, outside the scope of this study. In assessing the strength of training in terms of a clear sense of boundaries and a sense of received rewards, consistency is a very strong feature.

Boundaries

We have identified three questions suitable for measuring the respondents' sense of the boundaries in the agency:

- Are there service goals aimed at meeting customer expectations? *(Service goals)*

- Are there well-defined systems for linking customers' feedback and complaints to employees who can act on the information? *(Feedback)*

- Are you clear about how "good performance" is defined in your organization? *(Clear standards)*

The first simply identifies whether the bureaucrats are aware of the messages their supervisors communicate. It makes little sense to speak of the mobilizing role of the supervisors without also attending to whether the mobilization actually mobilizes. The evidence here is reasonably strong. If one groups the strongly agree and agree together, then those who agreed with the *Supervisor organizes* question were also somewhat more likely to agree with *Service goals:* 46 percent agreed in 1998, 42 percent agreed in 1999, and 43 percent agreed in 2000. The remainder of the observations were much more likely to fall in the off-diagonal cells.

The second question examines whether the bureaucrats are able to identify appropriate mechanisms for resolving customer complaints. Again, notice the service sector orientation in the reference to customers, which probably conveys something about at least the survey organizers' preferences for how one should regard average citizens. This is important because typical citizen complaints are numerous: the bureaucracy is too slow, makes arbitrary choices, makes choices that the citizen cannot accept, and so forth. But by this view, citizens set the boundaries of appropriate bureaucratic behavior.

The third question looks to the bureaucrats' assessment of the activities a bureaucrat might engage in and the prospective rewards for those activities.

Table 2.2 presents the marginals for the three surveys of federal employees. Here, there is some very small motion from 1998 to 2000. Without a doubt, the federal employees enthusiastically endorse the premise that there are service goals aimed at meeting customers' expectations. Between 66 and 75 percent of the respondents either agreed or strongly agreed with

Table 2.2   Distribution of Sense of Boundaries, Office of
Personnel Management

		SD	D	N	A	SA
Service goals	1998	3.3	9.6	12.9	51.7	22.5
	1999	4.6	11.8	16.8	48.9	17.8
	2000	5.1	10.8	20.2	46.4	17.5
Feedback	1998	7.7	25.7	23.3	33.9	9.5
	1999	9.1	25.5	24.4	32.6	8.4
	2000	10.3	23.4	27.2	30.0	9.1
Clear standards	1998	22.9	23.1	28.0	19.6	6.4
	1999	22.3	23.3	27.2	20.0	7.2
	2000	19.4	22.4	27.8	22.0	8.4

Source: Authors' compilation from 1998 to 2000 National Partnership for Reinventing Government Employee Surveys.
Note: Cell entries are the percentage either "strongly disagreeing" (SD), "disagreeing" (D), "neither agreeing nor disagreeing" (N), "agreeing" (A) or "strongly agreeing" (SA) with the question. Sample sizes were 13,689 in 1998, 18,154 in 1999, and 31,975 in 2000. All surveys were probability samples drawn to represent the universe of federal employees.

the statement, and only about 20 percent disagreed. Note that this construction of the boundaries is not punitive, but emphasizes the positive accomplishments of the subordinates. A more cynical reading of exactly the same question might be as follows: there are service goals, I don't meet them, therefore I don't meet customers' expectations.

For this question, and perhaps this one alone, there is, however, arguably a small drift downwards in the proportion who agree. Whereas 74.2 percent of the federal survey respondents agreed with the presence of service goals in 1998, only 66.7 percent agreed in 1999 and 63.9 percent in 2000. A 10 percent point drop is worrisome, if it in fact persists.

The percentage of federal employees who agree with the presence of feedback in their organization, however, holds largely flat over the three years of the survey. About 30 percent agreed with the feedback question in 1998, and a nearly equal 30 percent agreed in 2000.

If there is any improvement in these numbers—and it is so small that it borders on the trivial—it is that there is a small up-tick in the percentage of the respondents who agree that clear standards guide the distribution of merit-based rewards in the agency.

Note that none of these three questions deals with a punitive aspect of supervision: instead, all emphasize the supervisor's articulation of positive goals and the accomplishment of clear levels of performance. We will see a different story about boundaries in the section on social workers.

When it comes to boundaries, and unlike the marginals for training presented in figure 2.1, figure 2.2 indicates that no agencies, except possibly Food Safety, stand out from the rest in any consistent way. Two, however,

Figure 2.2   Respondents' Report of Boundaries

Agency	Values
OPM	08 9
Social Security	98
Small Business	8 0
NASA	089
GSA	8 9
FEMA	80
EEOC	890
EPA	089
Other Veterans	8 0
VBA	80
VHA	9 0 8
Other Treasury	80
Financial Management	8 90
Customs	9 08
IRS	8
Other Transportation	8
FAA	08 9
Other State	08 9
Bureau of Consular Affairs	809
Other Labor	809
OSHA	98
Other Justice	80
INS	8
Other Interior	980
National Park Service	98
HUD	8
Other HHS	80
Administration for Children and Families	80
HCFA	890
FDA	80
Energy	908
Other Education	80
Office of Post Secondary Education	0 8
Other Commerce	890
International Trade Association	8
Census	8
Patent and Trademark	80
NOAA	89
Other Agriculture	98
Food and Consumer	8 09
Animal and Plant Health	0 8
Food Safety	90 8
Forest Service	908
Other Defense	8 09
Defense Logistics	98
Navy	98 0
Army	980
Air Force	80

Source: Authors' compilation from 1998 to 2000 National Partnership for Reinventing Government Employee Surveys, Office of Personnel Management.

do stand out in terms of articulated service goals: the Bureau of Consumer Affairs and the Patent Office. Nonetheless, as service providers to the general public, both agencies are atypical. One agency stands out as a low performer: the Immigration and Naturalization Service (INS). We hesitate to offer a general argument about why these agencies are different. Indeed, the more general pattern is one of consistency.

The measures of strength of feedback, on an agency-by-agency basis, are again strikingly consistent. There is one positive outlier, the Bureau of Consular Affairs, which is again a very service oriented agency. Again, INS fares poorly in ratings of the quality of feedback, as does the Bureau of Food Safety.

Last, the measures of whether the agency allocated rewards on the basis of clear standards resurrects several familiar names. Health Care Financing Administration (HCFA) is again a low performer, and both Consular Affairs and the Patent Office clearly high performers.

Rewards

The three surveys provided us with six questions that reflected different aspects of the kinds of rewards that subordinates may have perceived.[2] We do wish to emphasize that rewards may be more than merely pecuniary. Indeed, several of the questions will be entirely neutral about the nature of the rewards. Surely rewards also include general job satisfaction, recognition from others, or beliefs that one's opinion makes a difference to the functioning of the organization.

- Are recognition and rewards based on merit?

- Are creativity and innovation rewarded?

- Are employees rewarded for working together in teams (for example, performance ratings, cash awards, certificates, public recognition)?

- Considering everything, how satisfied are you with your job?

- How satisfied are you with your involvement in decisions that affect your work?

- How satisfied are you with the recognition you receive for doing a good job?

The first question asks directly about recognition and obliquely about rewards. Recognition, which we would view as a solidary reward,[3] may be tied instead to material rewards of some kind (for example, a pay increase or time-off) or nothing more than peer acknowledgment.

The second question asks whether creativity and innovation are rewarded, but does not indicate by whom (peers, immediate supervisors, the agency as a whole) or about the locus of innovation. Presumably, innovation in some organizations may represent a problem more than a solution—in production agencies (Wilson 1989), where the purpose of the organization is more akin to factories that deliver constrained services, what kinds of innovation would actually constitute improvements?

The third question is much more specific about mechanisms, inquiring whether the employees believe that their participation on teams is welcome to agency management. There are, of course, reasons supervisors may prefer that subordinates not produce in teams—solo production reduces the costs of monitoring and increases the identifiability of individual contributions to policy production. Team production may increase the ultimate efficiency, however, if perhaps only under very specific and narrow conditions (Jensen and Meckling 1976; for more on production by teams, see Holmström 1982a, Miller 1992).

The fourth through sixth questions ask about job satisfaction. The fourth, in considering everything, thus explicitly combines pecuniary, functional, solidary, and incidental preferences. The fifth relates to functional preferences and the satisfaction the employee derives from contributions to decision making. The sixth related to solidary preferences and the satisfaction the employee derives from recognition on the job, presumably from peers as well as from the supervisory staff.

Table 2.3 presents the marginals for all six questions. There is an interesting divergence between the results for the first three (sources of satisfaction) and those for the last three (achieved satisfaction). The first three might lead one to conclude a very mixed, if not negative, picture of the accomplishments of the federal bureaucracy. The latter three, however, imply that federal bureaucrats are largely satisfied with their jobs on many dimensions.

Consider the first question, whether employees see rewards as being allocated by merit. Approximately 40 percent, in all three years, would tend to disagree. We would generally believe that this would be discouraging for the employees. It is, of course, a disadvantage of the survey method that we did not follow up these questions to discover what does determine the allocation of rewards. Is it simply seniority (and therefore something to which all bureaucrats are equally eligible, given enough time on the job)? Or is it favoritism (and thus something that would stir up greater feelings of unfairness)?

The proportions agreeing that either creativity or team-effort yield rewards are similar, and similarly discouraging. Again, about 40 percent of the federal employees tend to disagree that either creativity or team-effort are rewarded by the federal bureaucracy (and, again, these percentages are essentially flat across the three years of the study).[4]

Yet despite the attenuation of these inputs, the federal bureaucrats report relatively high levels of job satisfaction. In the fourth question,

Table 2.3   Distribution of Rewards, Office of Personnel Management

		SD	D	N	A	SA
Rewards by merit	1998	21.0	22.4	22.2	28.7	5.7
	1999	20.9	22.2	20.9	29.3	6.7
	2000	19.1	20.5	21.6	31.3	7.6
Creativity rewarded	1998	17.8	24.5	26.2	26.1	5.5
	1999	17.6	25.7	25.8	25.3	5.6
	2000	17.1	25.2	26.2	25.5	6.0
Team effort rewarded	1998	17.9	23.0	19.8	30.4	8.8
	1999	17.3	23.3	19.5	31.0	8.9
	2000	17.9	21.4	20.2	30.7	9.8
Satisfied with job	1998	8.4	15.4	13.1	43.6	19.5
	1999	7.9	15.5	15.7	44.0	17.0
	2000	6.8	14.3	18.1	44.9	15.8
Satisfied with involvement	1998	13.5	21.4	16.2	35.4	13.5
	1999	13.3	22.4	19.2	33.8	11.4
	2000	13.5	21.4	22.9	32.2	10.0
Satisfied with recognition	1998	18.0	21.9	16.5	31.6	12.0
	1999	17.2	21.4	17.9	32.1	11.4
	2000	16.9	20.4	19.6	32.3	10.8

Source: Authors' compilation from the 1998 to 2000 National Partnership for Reinventing Government Employee Surveys.
Note: Cell entries are the percentage either "strongly disagreeing" (SD), "disagreeing" (D), "neither agreeing nor disagreeing" (N), "agreeing" (A) or "strongly agreeing" (SA) with the question. Sample sizes were 13,689 in 1998, 18,154 in 1999, and 31,975 in 2000. All surveys were probability samples drawn to represent the universe of federal employees.

when asked to consider everything, about 60 percent of the respondents did approve of their jobs, nearly 20 percent strongly so. Further, there is good evidence that involvement in decisions (a functional preference) and recognition (a solidary preference) figured in their thinking about the job. Of course, there are many inputs beyond the sole functional and sole solidary preference mentioned here—power, career stability, other material benefits (for example, health benefits)—but the general picture should be one that the federal employees are reasonably well satisfied.

Do the agency-by-agency results give us any clues as to which bureaucrats are better rewarded? Here, again, the rule is consistency, not variation year-by-year, but again, there are some very familiar names among the agencies. There are consistent low performers, according to the respondents themselves: OSHA, the Veterans' Health Administration (VHA), the FAA, and the INS. There are also some consistent high performers: NASA, the Environmental Protection Agency (EPA), the Bureau of Consular Affairs, and the Government Services Administration (GSA). One could speculate that three out of the four high rewarders are agencies where scientific research dominates much of the activity (NASA, EPA, GSA); indeed, if one were to look at the subscales, these are the agencies where "creativity and innovation" are more likely to be rewarded than the others.

The overall picture should be one in which federal workers report significant levels of training (in the form of clarification of boundaries), a modest degree of belief that such boundaries do determine the kinds of rewards that they would see, and varying degrees of belief in the importance of adherence to those boundaries for their own rewards. Nonetheless, the overall picture may mask considerable variation across agencies.

Social Workers

We were also able to explore many of these same scales with a data collection of our own. This involved a mail-back survey of North Carolina social workers, specifically, frontline employees and their supervisors. Because of North Carolina privacy guidelines, we could not survey the clients.

An interesting feature of social work in North Carolina is that the state delegates the provision of social services entirely to the county, including the design of the institution. In 1945, Herbert Simon criticized the scientific management school of administration for attributing far too much certainty to the specific form of a hierarchy in organizations (in his example, public health). His criticism was that sometimes organizations would be organized by clientele, sometimes by task, and sometimes by geography. North Carolina's 100 county departments of social services include hierarchies organized along all three forms.

We initially contacted the directors of each of the departments, thirty of whom agreed to participate. The reasons for refusal were varied: some were conducting their own surveys, some had recently completed surveys, some were going through reorganizations. The distribution of the counties was quite representative of the state, including urban, farm, mountain, industrial, and ocean counties. The directors supplied us with the list of the names of the employees and a mailing address.

We then drew a random sample from the lists of names, and sent a mail-back questionnaire to 1,000 social workers and case workers. Of these, 511 responded (a better response rate than most mail-backs, but lower than that for the earlier Durham study).[5]

Figure 2.3   Respondents' Report of Rewards

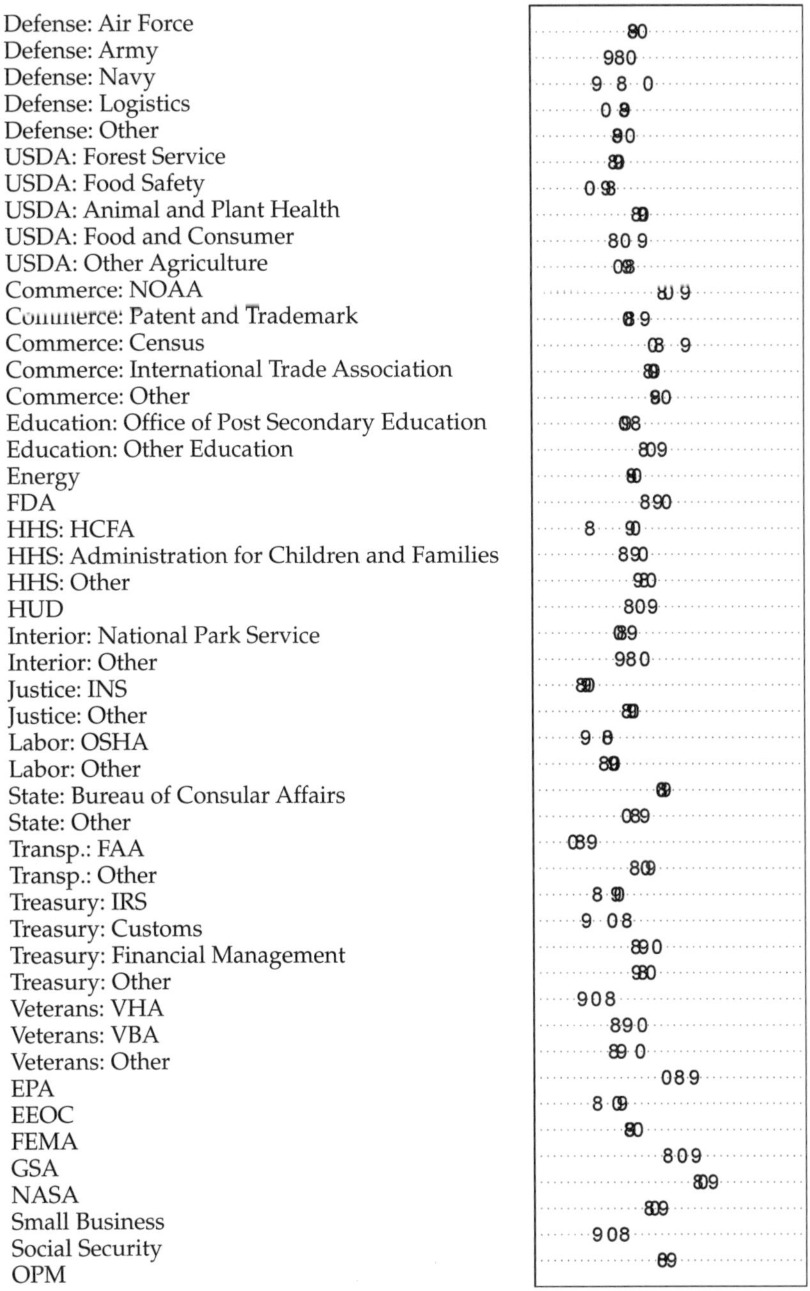

Agency	Values
Defense: Air Force	80
Defense: Army	980
Defense: Navy	9 8 0
Defense: Logistics	0 9
Defense: Other	90
USDA: Forest Service	89
USDA: Food Safety	0 98
USDA: Animal and Plant Health	89
USDA: Food and Consumer	80 9
USDA: Other Agriculture	098
Commerce: NOAA	80 9
Commerce: Patent and Trademark	89
Commerce: Census	08 9
Commerce: International Trade Association	89
Commerce: Other	80
Education: Office of Post Secondary Education	098
Education: Other Education	809
Energy	80
FDA	890
HHS: HCFA	8 90
HHS: Administration for Children and Families	890
HHS: Other	980
HUD	809
Interior: National Park Service	089
Interior: Other	980
Justice: INS	890
Justice: Other	89
Labor: OSHA	9 8
Labor: Other	89
State: Bureau of Consular Affairs	89
State: Other	089
Transp.: FAA	089
Transp.: Other	809
Treasury: IRS	8 9
Treasury: Customs	9 08
Treasury: Financial Management	890
Treasury: Other	980
Veterans: VHA	908
Veterans: VBA	890
Veterans: Other	89 0
EPA	089
EEOC	8 09
FEMA	80
GSA	809
NASA	809
Small Business	809
Social Security	908
OPM	89

Source: Authors' compilation from 1998 to 2000 National Partnership for Reinventing Government Employee Surveys, Office of Personnel Management.

Training

We asked four questions that would be relevant to the notion of training we are advancing in this chapter:

- Does your department invest a lot of time in training new employees?

- Does your department encourage you to attend seminars, classes, workshops, or conferences to keep abreast of advancements in your field?

- When you first came on the job, did you learn mainly from your supervisor and co-workers or on your own through trial and error? (one or the other)

- How much instruction did you receive from your supervisor when you first came on the job? (a lot, some, little, or none)

The first question simply records the social worker's assessment of the effort and resources the agency commits to training new employees. This corresponds to the time a supervisor devotes to supervision.

The second question notes the social worker's sense of the opportunities for training outside the immediate agency and is a reflection of the agency's commitment to training in best practices. Of course, best practices does not necessarily represent a committed reduction in the ambiguity of practices within the field, but it might. The best practice at any given time need not be the best practice some years hence.

The third question refers to the source of training: does it come from people within the organization (the supervisor or co-workers), or from the social worker's experience? Ideally, we should have asked a question that separated the sources of training (supervisors versus co-workers), though that is also perhaps somewhat unrealistic in terms of expectations about the respondent's ability to separate those sources, given that the successful supervisor would presumably also have co-workers who would echo the dicta of the supervisor.

The last question directly inquires about the supervisor's commitment of time and energy. It is, however, not at all clear what the optimal allocation of time would be. Imagine the most prescient and experienced employee: shouldn't the supervisor devote next to no time in supervision? And what would happen with workers who were decidedly recalcitrant? We expect none as the answer, and that only amenable subordinates would receive attention from the supervisors (see Brehm and Gates 1997, chap. 2).

Table 2.4 presents the marginals for the sense of training for this 2000 Survey of North Carolina Social Workers.

A majority of social workers (56 percent) did agree that the agency devoted a lot of time toward training. This distribution is not as skewed as

Table 2.4   Distribution of Sense of Training, North Carolina

	SD	D	N	A	SA
Training	.10	.21	.12	.36	.20
Classes	.06	.10	.12	.53	.20

	Supervisor	Self
Trial–Error	.4	.6

	A Lot	Some	Little	None
Supervisor Instruction	.26	.39	.28	.07

Source: Authors' compilation from the 2000 North Carolina Social Workers Survey.
Note: Captions refer to cell entries are the percentage either "strongly disagreeing" (SD), "disagreeing" (D), "neither agreeing nor disagreeing" (N), "agreeing" (A) or "strongly agreeing" (SA) with the question. Sample sizes were 511. All surveys were probability samples drawn to represent the universe of frontline North Carolina social workers.

that for the federal employees, in that a significant proportion (44 percent) disagreed.

The proportion who recognized external opportunities for training, however, is sizable at 73 percent. Of course, as noted, it is not clear what the supervisors' role is in these external opportunities, nor what kinds of ambiguity reduction take place.

More of the respondents (some 60 percent) felt that they learned the job on their own rather than from supervisors or from peers.

Last, the record of the supervisors with regard to the time the supervisor spends on training is mixed: only about a quarter of the respondents (26 percent) reported "a lot" of time and a very small fraction (7 percent) reported no time on training.

In sum, social workers view their supervisors as devoting some effort to direct supervision, but not an excessive amount. Supervisors are responsible for some of the caseload in many instances, thus simply do not have enough time to devote much to direct supervision. Moreover, as we have demonstrated in our earlier study (Brehm and Gates 1997, chap. 2, app. A), it is not appropriate for the supervisor to devote time and energy beyond the optimal—which can include both low performers who will not improve and high performers who do not need further intervention.

Boundaries

We used three questions to measure the respondents' sense of the boundaries of the organization:

- Is it easy to get fired if you don't do your job well?
- Are employees expected to follow orders without questioning?
- Are employees constantly checked for rule violations?

Table 2.5   Distribution of Sense of Boundaries, North Carolina

	SD	D	N	A	SA
Fired	.11	.36	.30	.20	.03
Follow orders	.25	.27	.37	.11	
Check rules	.06	.38	.25	.26	.05

Source: Authors' compilation from their 2000 North Carolina Social Workers Survey.
Note: Cell entries are the percentage either "strongly disagreeing" (SD), "disagreeing" (D), "neither agreeing nor disagreeing" (N), "agreeing" (A) or "strongly agreeing" (SA) with the question. Sample sizes were 511 in 2000. All surveys were probability samples drawn to represent the universe of frontline North Carolina social workers.

All three are put in very punitive terms. How well do these capture the capacities of the social workers to make sense of the boundaries in their ambiguous organizations? Despite the more punitive focus, it is clear from table 2.5 that the social workers did not see their jobs in that light. Although nearly half (47 percent) disagreed with the question about firing, nearly a quarter (23 percent) agreed. Similar fractions answer the question about following orders: a majority (52 percent) disagreed, only 11 percent agreed, and no one strongly agreed.

There is a tighter range of answers to the question about being constantly checked for rule violations. The distribution is slightly tilted toward disagreeing, but more fall in the disagree to agree bracket. Hardly any respondents held strong disagree or strong agree positions.

This does, of course, raise the question about how well the respondents pick up on the presence of the boundaries of the organization. Do social workers think in strictly punitive terms (for example, do this and you'll be fired, or, watch out for people looking over you), or is there a more positive and pro-active mode of supervision at work? The answer is outside the scope of our survey.

Rewards

We used four questions to explore the social workers' sense of the rewards of the job:

- Does this job provide you with a sense of accomplishment?
- Is the most rewarding part of this job that it really makes a difference?
- Does working hard at your job lead to respect from co-workers?
- Overall, how would you rate your satisfaction with your job on a scale where 1 means not at all satisfied and 5 means completely satisfied.

Table 2.6   Distribution of Sense of Rewards, North Carolina

	SD	D	N	A	SA
Job accomplishment	.03	.08	.11	.53	.24
Make difference	.03	.11	.24	.45	.17
Gain respect	.04	.13	.23	.50	.10

	Not Satisfied			Completely Satisfied	
Job satisfaction	.03	.11	.36	.44	.07

Source: Authors' compilation from the 2000 North Carolina Social Workers Survey.
Note: Cell entries are the percentage either "strongly disagreeing" (SD), "disagreeing" (D), "neither agreeing nor disagreeing" (N), "agreeing" (A) or "strongly agreeing" (SA) with the question. Sample sizes were 511 in 2000. All surveys were probability samples drawn to represent the universe of frontline North Carolina social workers.

The first two questions are squarely in the area of functional preferences: utility derived from achieving the purposes of the job itself. The third relates to solidary preferences: utility derived from the attitudes of others, particularly through recognition. The final question asks for a summary judgment about the social workers' state of satisfaction. The tabulation of the marginals for these questions appears in table 2.6.

The social workers report fairly strong levels of functional preferences: 77 percent agree or strongly agree with the question about accomplishment, 62 percent agree or strongly agree with the question about making a difference, and 60 percent report relatively high levels of solidary preferences as well.

All in all, the various utility streams translate into modest levels of job satisfaction: although only 7 percent report the highest level of satisfaction, nearly 50 percent report the next highest level.

The general picture across the three categories is consistent with, but does not confirm, the general argument. The respondents do report a fairly aggressive training program at work, involving the supervisor's time and attention as well as both direct and external training. The respondents, however, do not report that the punitive mode of training dominates. Functional and solidary preferences play a more significant role. In sum, the social workers seem generally satisfied.

Direct Effects of Training on Effort

Returning to the data on federal employees, we are able to estimate the direct effects of training upon effort. We propose a very simple endogenous core to the structure of this model, displayed in figure 2.4. This

Figure 2.4   Endogenous Core of Structural Equation Model

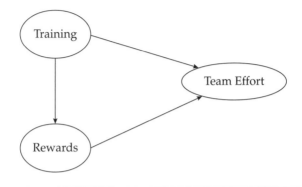

Source: Authors' compilation.

structural equations model treats two latent variables as endogenous: rewards, which are linked to training, and team effort, which is related to both rewards and training. This model treats training as endogenous to the system of equations. The key question is the basis on which we justify training as being causally prior to both rewards and effort.

One reason is that nearly every federal job entails some training before rewards are distributed and effort expended. There are explicit guidelines in the federal bureaucracy for what must be done where and when. Even paychecks come after a probationary period of training.

But another reason—only marginally sound—is that these models are not identified without a number of restrictions. This is what is referred to as a triangular model: training causally precedes rewards, which in turn precedes effort. None of the error terms associated with the latent variables are correlated, nor are any of the unique errors associated with the indicators. The reader is quite welcome to specify the model in a different form, and while we baldly assert that the structural model is appropriate, alternative specifications are certainly possible.

Table 2.7 displays our results. Training has both a direct and an indirect effect on team effort. Because the scale for training is fixed by the first loading, interpretation is relatively straightforward. A unit move on the scale for training, from neutral to strongly agree, corresponds to approximately a one-half move in the scale for performance, which in this analysis is team effort. Further, the indirect effect is likewise sizable: a move of one unit in the training scale corresponds to about a .2 movement in the performance scale. Altogether, a unit move in the training scale corresponds to nearly a .7 move in the scale for performance.

Table 2.7   Structural Equation Model Results, Office of
             Personnel Management

Variable	1998	1999	2000
Training → Team effort	.49	.53	.49
Rewards → Team effort	.45	.37	.42
Training → Rewards	.84	.83	.85

Source: Authors' compilation from 1998 to 2000 National Partnership for Reinventing Government Employee Surveys.
Note: All coefficients are statistically significant at $p < .01$ or beyond. Estimates are subsetted from the full structural equation model, where confirmatory factor loadings are presented in table 2.8.

What this implies is that training, conceived of as the clarification of the boundaries of acceptable behavior, exerts a powerful effect on assessments of team performance. To put the effects in perspective, the scales of the direct and indirect effects of training on performance is very close to that of a full unit. Measured across all forty-eight agencies, and with such consistency of the measurements (the factor loadings), this is very strong evidence for the role of training in cultivating team performance.

There is another effect worth addressing, namely, the direct effect of training on rewards. Although training nearly always falls behind rewards, this is also strong evidence that training yields rewards. Note that the rewards are not exclusively pecuniary. Recognition and job satisfaction are at least as important (Brehm and Gates 1997).

Discussion

Across these very different levels of analysis, then, we find strong evidence for a number of central points.

First, the employees are fully aware of supervisor efforts to train them, not in the sense of trying to make them like things that they don't really like, but of establishing what is acceptable and what is not. We have very strong evidence of efforts on the part of both federal and state-level supervisors to train subordinates. We also have very strong evidence of two meanings by which the subordinates could think about the boundaries. One direction, indicated by the social workers, fits with conventional ideas of supervision about boundaries: do this, and you'll be punished. The other direction, indicated by the federal employees, is much more positive: what does it take to do your job well?

Note the important difference between these two approaches: the former (tested on the social workers) emphasizes the coercive aspects

Table 2.8   Confirmatory Factor Scores, Office of Personnel Management

Variable	1998	1999	2000
Training scale			
Managers communicate the organization's mission, vision, and values	1.00	1.00	1.00
Employees receive training and guidance in providing high quality customer service	0.97	0.96	0.99
Employees receive the training they need to perform their jobs (for example, on-the-job training, conferences, workshops)	0.90	0.87	0.90
Are you clear about how "good performance" is defined in your organization?	0.94	0.94	0.92
Overall, how good a job do you feel is being done by your immediate supervisor or team leader?	0.42	0.41	0.44
Employees are required to report the hours they work on a daily basis	0.53	0.53	0.58
Effort scale			
A spirit of cooperation and teamwork exists in my immediate work unit	1.00	1.00	1.00
There are well-defined systems for linking customers' feedback and complaints to employees who can act on the information	0.86	1.02	1.04
Teams are used to accomplish organizational goals, when appropriate	0.98	1.11	1.08
My organization has made reinvention a priority (for example, working smarter and more efficiently)	0.85	1.00	1.01
In the past two years, the productivity of my work unit has improved	0.90	0.94	0.95
How would you rate the overall quality of work being done in your work group?	0.92	0.94	0.95
Recognition and rewards are based on merit	1.10	1.12	1.08
Creativity and innovation are rewarded	1.13	1.04	1.10
Rewards scale			
Employees are rewarded for working together in teams (for example, performance ratings, cash awards, certificates, public recognition)	1.00	1.00	1.00
Considering everything, how satisfied are you with your job?	1.00	1.04	0.98
How satisfied are you with your involvement in decisions that affect your work?	1.09	1.12	1.06
How satisfied are you with the recognition you receive for doing a good job?	1.11	1.14	1.10
Overall, how good a job do you feel is being done by your immediate supervisor or team leader?	0.59	0.63	0.57

Source: Authors' compilation from 1998 to 2000 National Partnership for Reinventing Government Employee Surveys.
Note: Coefficients are confirmatory factor loadings reported from the overall structural equation model. All coefficients are statistically significant at $p < .01$ or beyond.

of supervision, whereas the latter (tested with the federal employees) stresses the cooperative, ambiguity aspects of supervision.

We have no doubt whatsoever that supervisors in the federal system also need to engage in the more punitive aspects of boundary-setting, and that the supervisors in the state system must define roles more positively. At this early stage in our argument, we think it is essential that the reader attend to how the definition of boundaries within an agency performing in an ambiguous environment takes on both valences.

We also want to encourage the reader to heed the different utilities that the subordinates may associate with different outcomes. A narrow-minded focus on pecuniary or material benefits really misses the point, not just about what the subordinate bureaucrats appreciate about their jobs, but, critically, also about what bureaucratic supervisors might be able to press. Both the social workers and the federal bureaucrats (across a full range of agencies) report relatively high levels of job satisfaction, perhaps, but not definitively (in the least) stemming from their functional and solidary preferences. In other words, the job itself and colleagues matter most.

Chapter 3

Adapting Preferences

EARLY MANAGEMENT schemes, such as those mentioned in chapter 1, worried about characteristics of the division of labor between subordinates and supervisors that inhibited close supervision. Such scholars—especially Luther Gulick—debated optimum span of control, virtues of piece work, and scalar chains of command in the early twentieth century. In contemporary terminology, the principal may structure incentives or schemes of observation to overcome adverse selection and moral hazard.[1] These are classic examples of a coercive approach to management.

But here the literatures depart ways: organization theorists began to question whether supervisors could expect orders to be followed simply because they were given. Consider the words of Mary Parker Follett:

> To some men the matter of given orders seems a very simple affair; they expect to issue their own orders and have them obeyed without question. Yet, on the other hand, the shrewd common sense of many a business executive has shown him that the issuing of an order is surrounded by many difficulties; that to demand an unquestioning obedience to orders not approved, not perhaps even understood, is bad business policy (1926, 43).

To be sure, principal-agency theorists also question the likelihood of obedience given certain schemes of observation or structures of incentives, but there is a vital point of difference in the emergence of the human relations school of organization theory: supervisors are responsible for socializing their employees, help subordinates to discover appropriate courses of action. In other words, they teach. Teaching becomes especially relevant when agents operating in environments of great uncertainty must make decisions; supervisors in this way help inform subordinates as to what choices to make. In formalizing the idea that principals may divert some of their resources to teaching, our goal is to elaborate on the value of teaching to both principal and agent.

Some readers, particularly those from an economics background, might dismiss the project of this chapter as attempting to change the preferences of the subordinate. In the language of economics, preferences denote the ranking between alternatives. A colorful example was offered by a true believer in the field: I have always preferred good music. When I was fifteen, Black Sabbath was good music; now that I am adult, Mozart is good music. Economists even use a Latin phrase to justify their cause, *de gustibus non est disputandum*, there is no disputing taste.[2] But that really is not at all our goal or method here. Instead, we want to see what the effect of supervisor's resources devoted to teaching is on subordinate utility and effort. Does a diversion of extra resources cause subordinates to become happier at what they do?

Early dynamic agency models by Ariel Rubinstein (1979) and Roy Radner (1981) make a formal argument that, over the long term, principals can effectively deal with incentive problems; as the super-game progresses, hidden action problems diminish. These results should make sense: if the same type of person is acting in the same setting, then the problems of knowing what she is likely to do next should diminish. More specifically, focusing on the principal-agent relationship between owners and managers, Eugene Fama (1980) studies the role of the market as an automatic mechanism by which managers' market values are adjusted over time to reflect their work. Bengt Holmström (1982b) formalizes this argument with markets updating beliefs about a manager's competence and level of effort. Jean-Jacques Laffont and Jean Tirole (1988) challenge Holmström (1982b) in several ways, but the primary difference is that for Holmström an agent attempts to prove their productivity while for Laffont and Tirole the agent endeavors not to appear too productive. The Laffont and Tirole agent is worried about how high performance today will lead to a more demanding incentive scheme tomorrow, "the ratchet effect." Their model demonstrates that in a repeated relationship without commitment, it is difficult for principals to separate underproductive agents from genuinely productive agents, forcing principals to offer generous incentive schemes. Laffont and Tirole (1990, 618) compare models with varying degrees of commitment and discount rates. With a large discount factor, full commitment and commitment with renegotiation, principals are able to separate "good" and "bad" agents; with no commitment the equilibrium tends to be fully pooling.[3] What happens when the nature of the relationship between the principal and agent is modeled differently? What happens when we take into account teaching?

There is at least one other prominent version of a dynamic model of supervision in this language: William Bianco and Robert Bates (1990) offer an iterated production-by-teams game, distinguishing between limited and enhanced leaders (principals). Limited leaders resemble

Holmström's managers, who deal with the team as a whole (1982a). Enhanced leaders, on the other hand, can observe individual agents and are able to allocate residuals across agents. Whether a leader (principal) is able to attain organizational compliance depends on his or her capabilities (information regarding agent action). As with other models of agency, Bianco and Bates do not focus on the characteristics of agents. These dynamic models of agency analyze how principals discover information about agents over a series of interactions. Different models come to a variety of conclusions as to how successful principals will be at inducing compliance depending on a variety of factors, yet in none of these models is there any teaching whereby a principal serves to guide agents' choices. How does teaching affect the relationship between the principal and the agent?

Here we focus on the teaching of pro-social preferences (or organizational socialization) as well as learning by agents. Specifically, we model a dynamic principal-agent relationship, focusing on how teaching can alter agent values. Many principal-agent models explicitly deal with learning, but few, if any, incorporate teaching. Why focus on teaching in an organization? For many reasons, we argue that it is imperative to consider the implications of teaching in agency theory.

First, teaching is a way to explicitly account for formal and informal interactions in the workplace. In the day-to-day interactions between a supervisor and a subordinate, supervisors not only administer rewards and punishments but also convey information to subordinates about how to do their jobs. Some have argued that the teachers in a workplace are more effective supervisors than the taskmasters. For organizations as a whole, a focus on teaching helps explain the plethora of training sessions and workshops that are foisted on so many workers. Managers devote time and energy directly running workshops or setting up training sessions. Clearly, organizational principals see such programs as serving an obvious and useful purpose. Training sessions and workshops might mitigate the problems of adverse selection. Such programs do not necessarily reveal information about an agent's type, but inculcate a set of values and norms that fit an organization's culture. Thus they work to alter types. Coming from a different literature, Chester Barnard described this as a process of "subordinating individual interest . . . to the good of the cooperative whole" (1938/1968, 279). Successful teaching produces workers who share their supervisor's goals. Subordinates learn, but are also taught.

Second, teaching may be especially useful in environments of uncertain or ambiguous information. Agents often must make choices regarding complex policies. Dan Wood (1988), for example, examines conflict between EPA bureaucrats and presidents over the enforcement of the Clean Air Act. Mathew McCubbins, Roger Noll, and Barry Weingast

(1990) model the differing values of the Joint Committee on Atomic Energy and the Atomic Energy Commission for the promotion of nuclear power. Although it may be convenient to speak of the values of agents toward these complex policy domains, the policies themselves represent conflicts among other principles. We are skeptical that individuals, much less agencies, actively involved in policy making can have fixed values over such broad questions as interest rates, use of national forests, or energy generation. Higher interest rates benefit individuals on fixed incomes but are a curse to mortgage holders. Conservation of timber in national forests may benefit recreational users and environmentalists, but is a bane to loggers and ranchers. Coal plant power generation may tap into inexpensive (and for the United States, substantial) energy stores, but has its costs in air pollution and miners' health and welfare. Certainly, it is possible for some individuals to have very strong and fixed values about these questions. It is also quite reasonable to view these as policy quandaries, and that serious and sober individuals may have great difficulties sorting out their values over such complex policy domains. Teaching, in this respect, is the informal allocation of time and energy by a supervisor toward a subordinate to guide their policy choices.

Third, a focus on teaching helps to explain how organizations attempt to achieve a new working culture or adapt to a changing environment. If one adopts a view of organizations as participants in an enveloping environment, akin to the general systems theory popular in the 1950s and 1960s, the environment may compel changes to the organizations, including preference change for members of the organization. Again, from a more classic organization theory approach, Herbert Kaufman (1985) observes that, in response to environmental change, organizations might identify new supplies, adopt new methods of output, or alter organizational structure. These are also, unfortunately, chief among the reasons that organizations die. Teaching, in this way, serves as a tool for organizational adaptation.

Indeed, in a recent book, Bryan Jones articulates why individuals, and the organizations they inhabit, must be conceived as adaptive systems:

> When humans face a problem, we tend to solve it adaptively. We may do so directly, through a process of reasoning based on past experience or learning, or we may do so through the development of better and better designs over time, designs that are stored in memory for future use. Only a few human characteristics will limit our ability to adapt to the problem solving environment, but these characteristics are critical. . . . These limiting characteristics correspond to E. O. Wilson's epigenetic rules—or, rather, they are those epigenetic rules that may have been adaptive at one time or may still be adaptive in a different place, but are not relevant to the current problem-solving task (2001, 33–34).

Epigenetic rules are, roughly, the trade-offs between preparedness and deliberation, where preparedness denotes hardwired decision rules, whereas deliberation denotes our capacity to switch among those rules. We are an adaptive species, operating within adaptive organizations, but there are knowable limits to our adaptation.

Further, political scientists typically treat entire organizations as if they were solitary principals or agents. Yet, if we regard the goals of the entire organization as some aggregation of individual values, then any change to the composition of the organization means that the values of the organization itself have changed. We can not eliminate the problem of the aggregation of values by simply defining some particular organizational goal. Richard Cyert and James March (1963) elaborate on the problems of producing a common goal from individual values, noting that such goals are more often aspirations devoid of substance than concrete plans for action (see also Wilson 1989, 32–36).[4] Further, the problem of aggregating individual values is an intrinsic component of agency theory itself in the adverse selection problem. Unless we are willing to wave off adverse selection, principals within the organization cannot be certain that individuals they hire and promote will have values consonant with the organization. Teaching plays a role in shaping organizational goals through its effect on individuals. It may change dispositions even as it provides information in a complex environment.

To model the effect of teaching, we are influenced by a variety of learning theories. Economists utilize a variety of distinct approaches to understand how individuals learn to prefer some alternatives over others. One approach considers values as revealed to oneself over the course of experience. Richard Cyert and Morris DeGroot (1975) consider the essential preferences to be fixed, but unknown. New experiences allow individuals to identify what they like or dislike. Dynamic models of principal-agent relationships follow this approach. This perspective is applied to work on dynamic principal-agent problems and incomplete contracts, where contracts are renegotiated. The model we present here differs from this approach in that we focus our attention on how teaching affects the behavior and dispositions of agents.

Athanasios Orphanides and David Zervos (1995) posit a learning model of addiction with regret. Unlike other rational models of addiction (see Stigler and Becker 1977; Becker and Murphy 1988), Orphanides and Zervos incorporate regret into their analysis. That is, over time, addicts may learn to regret their addiction. Such a model of regret allows education to play a role in discouraging addiction. Yet education is only seen to be valuable as a source of information. Teaching itself is not modeled. In contrast, our model examines the allocation of teaching and how subordinates respond to teaching.

The more explicit influence comes from Michael Cohen and Robert Axelrod (1984), who model preference change as directly affecting utility for individuals. In their model of a manager coping with a misspecified production function, the manager who adapts is everywhere better off than the manager who heels to strict preferences. Similarly, artificial intelligence methods for winning complex games like checkers, chess, or Go might rely on points marking fixed values over for certain configurations of the board games, but the more successful programs adapt the values of different configurations. The classic example of machine learning is Arthur Samuel's checker player (1959), renowned for defeating state champions in the 1950s and 1960s. We explicitly draw on these learning models, but focus our attention more particularly on the teaching process.

We are not arguing that individuals change their preferences in irrational directions, or that principals have unlimited abilities to change theirs. We would not make the claim that we could eliminate the problems of poverty simply by teaching people to prefer not having money. Even though our chapter accords very strong abilities to the principal, as the reader will see, the agents' preferences change only in directions that are consonant, never dissonant, with original preferences.

We offer a very simple model of an agent whose utility for different outcomes is affected by a principal's investment in teaching. Teaching thereby alters utilities. Because the complexities of even this very simple model prohibit a closed-form solution, we apply computer simulation to produce a numerical solution and identify the results of teaching and learning for both principal's and agent's utilities.

A Dynamic Principal-Agency Model with Teaching and Learning

Our model begins with a principal contracting for work from a single agent who has N activities.[5] The principal's utility values for each activity forms a vector p of length N, where p_i is the principal's utility for activity i. The agent puts effort a_i into activity i at time t, with the total effort normalized to 1:

$$\sum_{i=1}^{N} a_{it} = 1; \quad 0 \le a_{it} \le 1 \tag{3.1}$$

The principal's utilities for different outcomes are fixed. The principal's utility might be positive (reflecting work), zero (reflecting shirking, or non-work), or negative (reflecting sabotage, or nonproductive work). Hence, an agent might be putting effort into not working or even to undermining production. In this manner we move beyond a simple work-shirk dichotomy typical of most principal-agent models.[6]

The utility to the principal is simply the product of the vectors for the principal's utility values and the agent's effort, less any residual (R_t) amount the principal decides to redistribute to the agent:

$$U_{p_t} = p'a_t - R_t \qquad (3.2)$$

The principal's chief method to gain compliance (productive work) from the agent is the distribution of the residual as either a "reward" (r_t) or as an investment in "teaching" (d_t). (Both r_t and d_t are vectors of length N.) Further, the principal may distribute only those residuals the agent actually produces.

$$R_t = r_t + d_t \leq p'a_t \qquad (3.3)$$

The agent's expected utility is a function of the value agent assigns to particular outcome, effort, and any reward dispensed back to the agent:

$$U_{a_t} = a_t'w_t + r_t \qquad (3.4)$$

where w_t is a vector of length N where each element w_{it} describes the agent's utility for activity i at time t.

The principal may teach the agent by investing d_t in a short-term teaching component for the agent. The agent's realized utility is similar to the expected utility, except augmented by teaching:

$$\hat{U}_{a_t} = \left(w_t + f\left(d_t\right)\right)' a_t + r_t \qquad (3.5)$$

where the function $f(d_t)$ represents some temporary change due to the teaching investment. The function may return either a vector or a scalar. Of course, there are an infinite number of ways we might represent the effect of teaching. In the present context, we let teaching be a deterministic relationship between a new parameter, the teaching efficiency (E, a scalar) and the amount spent (that is, returning a vector):

$$f\left(d_t\right) = d_t \times E \qquad (3.6)$$

It would be possible to represent teaching as a more probabilistic function as well. For reasons that should become clear in the subsequent section on results of this model, even this very charitable view of the capacities of the principal to teach is surprisingly limited. Were we to move to a probabilistic teaching function, we would expect that the effect of teaching would be more constrained than teaching in a deterministic function.

The machine learning models, as well as Cohen and Axelrod's of the adapting manager, rely on surprise as the chief agent of change. Such surprises are, of course, more evident in environments of high uncertainty. Formally, we express surprise (D_t) as the difference between reality and expectations:

$$D_t = U_{a_t} - \hat{U}_{a_t}$$
$$= -d_t' a_t d_t \times E \tag{3.7}$$

The function describing the agent's response to teaching must fulfill several important criteria. The function has to be sensitive to the context of previous changes in effort. The idea is that the agent's utility values refer to the effort that agent's put into various activities, and that the principal should be able to induce long-term utility change by short-term changes in the utility associated with a particular outcome due to teaching. The agent's response to teaching has to be weighted with respect to previous efforts if it is to prevent run away changes to utilities. Cohen and Axelrod (1984) offer the following function, which we unabashedly borrow:

$$w_{i,t+1} = w_{it} + \frac{a_{it} - a_{i,t-1}}{|a_{it}|} \cdot \frac{D_{it}}{a_{it}} \tag{3.8}$$

The final component of this model is a system for the agent's behavior to change. Here, again, there is an infinite array of possible adaptation functions for behavior, but we operationalize behavior change with a simple linear learning model (Lave and March 1975). If the agent's behavior was rewarded (relative to the agent's utility), the agent is more likely to continue that behavior than in the past. Conversely, if the agent's behavior was punished (relative to the agent's utility), the agent should be less likely to continue that behavior in the future. We require that rewards and punishment operate with respect to the agent's utilities because it is not plausible that agents would continue rewarded actions if they received a utility for defecting that was greater than the reward. Define Z as the agent's responsiveness to reward (risk-taking and risk-aversion). The specific function is as follows:

$$\text{If } (r_{it} + w_{it} \leq 0): a_{i,t+1} = a_{it} + Z(1 - a_{it})$$
$$\text{If } (r_{it} + w_{it} \leq 0): a_{i,t-1} = a_{it} - Za_{it} \tag{3.9}$$

The problem for the principal is to maximize U_{pt} subject to these different functions and constraints. What is the principal's optimum allocation of investment to teaching relative to reward? To the best of our knowledge, there is no closed-form solution to this problem. As with most learning models, the final equilibrium of the agent's effort and utility depends

Figure 3.1   Flowchart for Teaching and Learning Simulation

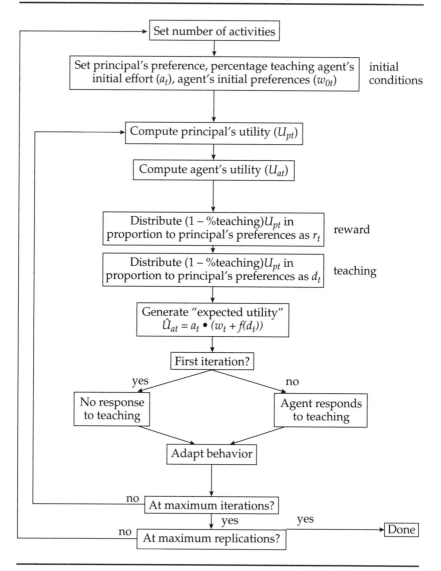

Source: Authors' compilation.

utterly on initial conditions, a general feature of nonlinear models. Fortunately, computers make a numerical solution possible. We thus use a computer simulation of this model to derive our results. The flowchart for the model appears in figure 3.1. The source code (in Java) is available from the authors on request. We now turn to a discussion of the results.

Results of a Simulation of the Model

To simplify the explication of our model, we operationalize the number of activities as three: working, shirking, and sabotage. The distinction between the activities derives from our own earlier work on the enhanced principal-agent model (Brehm and Gates 1994, 1997). Whereas effort expended in work results in positive utility for the principal, effort in shirking results in no gain for the principal, and sabotage leads to negative utility.[7] To further simplify the analysis, we let the principal's utility values be {−1,0,1} to denote utility of sabotage, shirking, and working respectively.

We let the agent's initial utility values vary from −1 to 1 across all three activities and the agent's initial effort vary from 0 to 1. As a variance reducing step, we fix the agent's responsiveness to reward (risk-taking and risk-aversion) to be .3, which is well within the range of typical utility for this parameter.[8] One further variance reduction step became obvious after the first applications of the simulation: the responsiveness of the principal's utility to the efficiency of teaching is negligible. We fix the parameter for teaching efficiency at 200 percent, or that every dollar spent on teaching resulted in a 200 percent change in attitudes, in the short run. The simulation runs over twenty iterations in each of 100 replications, yielding a data set with 2000 observations.

Our first point of concern is to ask what happens to the principal's utility over time. Figure 3.2 displays the change to the principal's utility over each successive iteration. The trilobite-like scatterplot implies that the principal may sometimes fare extremely well (tend toward 1), sometimes fare very poorly (tend toward −1), and sometimes not gain anything (tend toward 0). Surely these results have echoes in empirical observations of organizations in that some organizations excel while others flounder, perhaps even with the same management techniques. Any model suggesting that an organization would succeed were it only to do X, Y, and Z would have its imitators. Management is not as simple as that.

What, then, accounts for the final point of convergence for the principal's utility? The answer becomes apparent only through some graphical detective work. What matters are the agent's initial predispositions toward all three activities, and, specifically, only when the agent is positively inclined toward work in the first place.

Indeed, the only time the principal can be assured of positive net utility is when the agent prefers to work and has negative utilities about both shirking and sabotage. Figure 3.3 shows a scatterplot in which each iteration brings rapidly accelerating positive utility for the principal.

Figure 3.2   Principal's Utility over Iterations for All Conditions

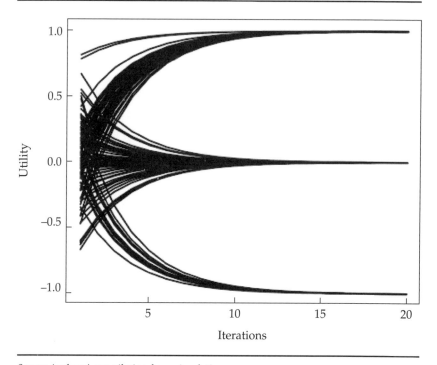

Source: Authors' compilation from simulations.

These results are entirely consistent with our arguments about the singular importance of the agent's preferences in the principal-agent problem (Brehm and Gates 1993, 1994, 1997). Principal-agent models conventionally treat the agent's preferences as contrary to those of the principal, but one should hardly regard it as a truth. Indeed, in our study of working and shirking by police officers (Brehm and Gates 1993), civil servants, and social workers (Brehm and Gates 1997), we found that the best predictors of the subordinate's nonshirking behavior were functional and solidary attachments to the job.

These results are also, in part, related to the traditional notion of redistributing residual profits, a central theme of principal-agent models. In the public sector, without profits or residuals as traditionally conceived, we can think of residuals for the supervisor to redistribute as rewards.[9] For the supervisor to have some residual to redistribute, he or she must have had some net positive payoff from his or her subordinate. When does he or she have a net positive payoff in the present scenario? When the agent puts more effort into work than into sabotage. Suppose that the

Figure 3.3   **Principal's Utility over Iterations Given Negative Predispositions Toward Shirking and Sabotage, and Positive Predispositions Toward Work**

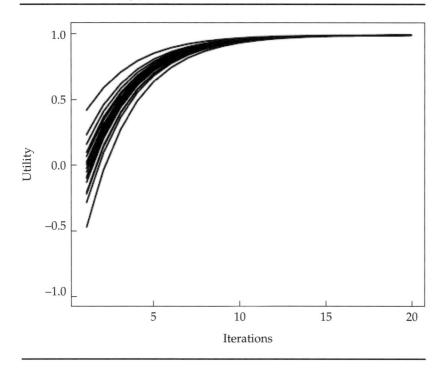

Source: Authors' compilation from simulations.

agent prefers sabotage ($w_{10} > 0$). It is only when rewards are greater than the agent's preferences toward sabotage that the agent can be taught to reduce effort toward sabotage. One variation of the model that might be of interest as a potential escape from the principal's inability to redistribute residuals when there isn't any initial production is to allow the principal to borrow from an external source. Without initial compliance and external sources of residuals to redistribute, the principal is stymied. When there is a modest initial level of compliance, the principal can improve on the compliance with the appropriate distribution of the residuals.

What is the appropriate distribution of residuals over reward and percent devoted toward teaching? The answer surprised us, because we expected that there would be at least some region where it was more profitable to teach than to bribe, and vice versa. Figure 3.4 demonstrates the relationship between the principal's utility at the final iteration (by

Figure 3.4   Distribution of Residuals

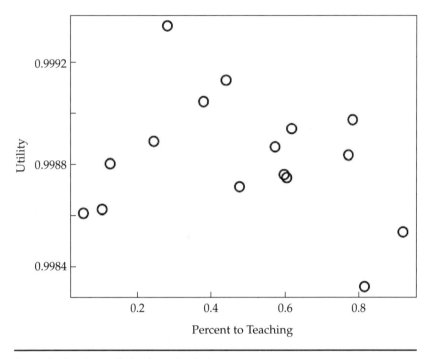

Percent to Teaching

Source: Authors' compilation from simulations.

convergence) and the percentage of the residual that the principal devotes to teaching. The scatterplot is flat: the principal gains no leverage by distributing the residuals one way or another. We have further comment on this surprising result in later paragraphs when we discuss the relationship between the amount that the principal devotes to teaching and the agent's preferences.

Where does the gain for the principal come from? His or her preferences, after all, remain fixed for this model—only the agent adapts. The principal's utility must come from changes to the agent's level of effort across the three activities. In figure 3.5, we display the rate of change in the agent's efforts at sabotage over time. One would see virtually identical plots for the rate of change in the agent's efforts at shirking or work as well. The pattern tends toward one of two extremes, devoting either 0 or 100 percent of one's activities toward sabotage. If one disentangles the plots, one shouldn't be surprised to see very much the same relationship we uncovered for the effect of initial predispositions: by the final iteration, agents learn to devote 100 percent of their

Figure 3.5   Change in Agent Effort at Sabotage

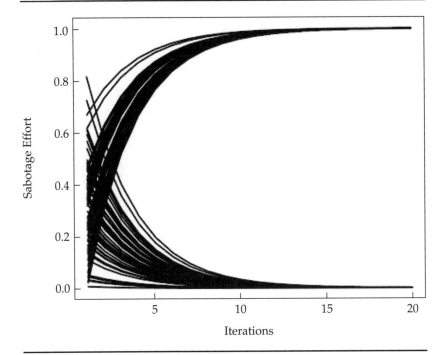

Source: Authors' compilation from simulations.

time to the activities that yield the most to them in terms of their initial preferences.

If we confine our examination of the responsiveness to teaching and the change in the agent's orientation for work to those cases when the agent has a positive predisposition to work, the story is quite different. Figure 3.6 demonstrates the dynamics of the agent's preferences given a positive initial preference toward work. The pattern is something of a gray smear, though a superficial examination identifies that there is an upward curve to the agent's preferences over time, if with a very slight slope in many circumstances. The implication is that when agents prefer to work, the principal has a modest capacity to enhance those preferences. We see a positive response to teaching.

The principal can improve markedly on the agent's preferences when there are further constraints (see figure 3.7). If the agent initially prefers to work, and has negative preferences for shirking and sabotage (i.e., w_{10}, $w_{20} < 0$, $w_{30} > 0$), the principal has a much greater effect on the agent's preferences.

Figure 3.6   Agent's Preferences for Work Given Supervisor Exhibits Positive Predisposition Toward Work

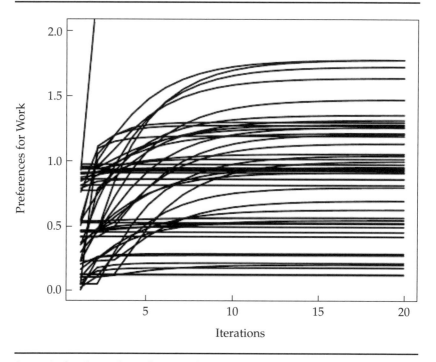

Source: Authors' compilation from simulations.

Although the percentage that the principal devotes to teaching has little effect on his or her own utility, it has a sharp and significant effect on the agent's utility. Figure 3.8 demonstrates the relationship between the agent's preferences toward work at the final iteration as a function of teaching. There is a modest, if noisy, upwards slope to the scatterplot. The more that the principal devotes to teaching, the more positive the agent's preferences become toward work. The relationship is further accentuated when one looks at figure 3.9, the scatterplot of the agent's utility from work and the percentage that the principal devotes to teaching.

This final result, in juxtaposition to the nonresult on the effect of teaching for the principal's utility, is one we take to be quite important. In a way, this model represents both the entry into and the exit from the so-called human relations school of organization theory. Chester Barnard (1938/1968), Elton Mayo (1945), and others suggested that subordinate obedience to supervisors' orders, as well as the net

Figure 3.7   Agent's Preferences for Work over Iterations Given
Supervisor: Positive Predispositions Toward Work, Negative
Predispositions Toward Shirking and Sabotage

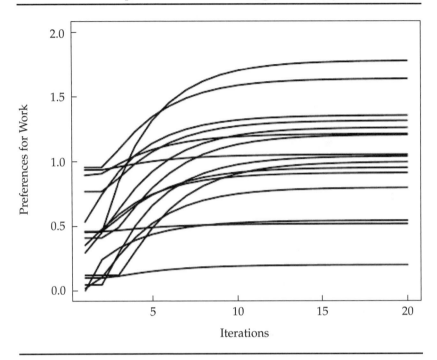

Source: Authors' compilation from simulations.

productivity of the firm, depended on the attitudes of subordinates
toward their jobs. As a result, many companies launched experimental programs to encourage subordinates to favor company goals, boost
worker morale and allegiance to the company. Few of the programs
succeeded in terms of long-term changes to worker productivity.
Workers may have become happier because of the efforts of the human
relations programs, but the net utility to the principals remained much
the same.

The stories of the human relations programs resonate in our model
of adaptive preferences. If the sole criterion on which to evaluate a
program is the net gain it has for the principal (by increasing production), then our model suggests that investment in teaching is of little
or no effect on the productivity of the agent. But if the agent's utility
is a criterion in its own right, then our model suggests that it is possible
for teaching to improve the utility of the agents.

Figure 3.8   Agent's Preferences for Work as a Function of Percent
              to Teaching

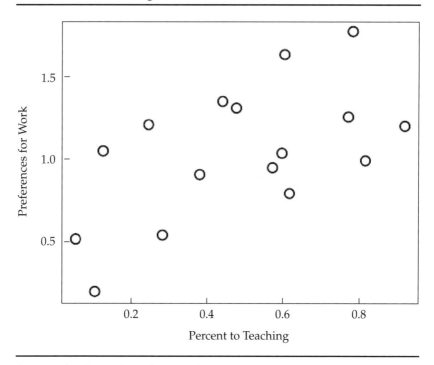

Source: Authors' compilation from simulations.

Perhaps, also, mainstream welfare economists should be happy with
the outcome of these results. After all, if we could teach people that
war, starvation, and poverty were desirable things, then none of the three
would really constitute problems. Again, the core result is that though
principals can make agents happier, they cannot be ensured of greater
effort on the part of the agents.

Discussion

Agency theory encourages students of organizations to think about the
interplay between the asymmetry of information between principal and
agent, and the structures of the organization that mitigate adverse selection and moral hazard. Some recent portrayals of successful principals
identify sources of their success in the nature of supervision, the predispositions of the subordinates, commitment, discount rates, and the
distribution of residuals. Our findings speak directly to the plausibility

Figure 3.9   Agent's Utility from Work as a Function of Percent
to Teaching

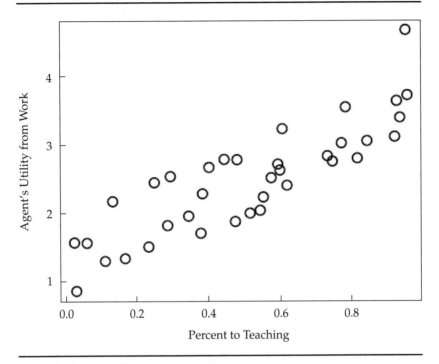

Source: Authors' compilation from simulations.

of these different sources. More specifically, we examine the role teaching plays in altering behavior and how this affects the relationship between principals and agents.

The most general conclusion is that the results of our simulations parallel the notions of a pooling and separating equilibrium found in Laffont and Tirole (1988, 1990). In terms of our conceptualization, Laffont and Tirole's ratcheting problem involves agents who are predisposed to produce output, but not at the level desired by the principal. Our results, on the other hand, run directly against the central conclusion of much of the work on dynamic models of agency. The conclusion presented by Ariel Rubinstein (1979), Roy Radner (1981), and others is that, in the long run, hidden action problems are unveiled allowing principals to construct appropriate incentive mechanisms. Our results tend to not support this conclusion.

Bianco and Bates (1990) argue that the principal (a leader in their nomenclature) endowed with the ability to target rewards to agents on the basis of individual performance may be able to sustain cooperation.

Conversely, principals who cannot target rewards on the basis of individual contributions are significantly hampered in their efforts. Although it is understated in their original article, principals must have initial cooperation from the agents to proceed to sustained cooperation: the principal's great strength is an ability to initiate cooperation in the first iteration. We suggest a stronger condition: principals must have agents with positive attitudes toward work in the first place. Our condition is more stringent because it is possible that the agents in the Bianco and Bates model could accidentally cooperate against their initial preferences. Without a positive initial contribution from the agent, the principal does not have a residual to redistribute, and cannot solicit enhanced levels of cooperation.

Have we just dissolved the principal-agency problem by saying that if principals and agents favor the same ends, then principals have little difficulty in persuading agents to achieve them? Not at all. Recall that the agent in our model has both variable effort and variable preferences. As long as the agent's preferences are marginally positive toward work, the principal can use the net production to stimulate greater effort. Under our model, the agent's preferences toward work are at the start less than those of the principal. The agent, however, may come to prefer work more than the principal. Interestingly, in this case, these results are more optimistic than those of Laffont and Tirole (1988).

Although the utility for the principal is not improved by extra efforts toward teaching, the utility for the agent can be. There is a direct relationship between the agent's final preferences toward work and the principal's effort. If the bottom line of the principal-agency game is to boost the principal's utility (that is, increase production), principals do not gain from teaching. As Charles Perrow (1986) writes in his blistering criticism of agency theory, this is an excessively conservative view of the purpose of organizations. If one sees organizations as opportunities for agents to engage in productive work and to acquire positive utility from their work, our model argues that teaching the agent can have enduring effects on the agent's utility from such work.

PART II

TASK MANAGEMENT

Chapter 4

Task Allocation in Public Bureaucracies

A S SHOULD be becoming evident after reading this far, organization theorists are consistent in their argument that the coercive aspects of supervision in public bureaucracies alone cannot account for high levels of performance. Indeed, this point may have been ascertained by the reference to Barnard (1938/1968) in the subtitle of this book. Like those of the private sector executive, the functions of the public executive are many. Although coercion, in the form of the application of rewards and sanctions for performance, deters shirking and encourages working, it is a pale and limp tool for the supervisor seeking to generate significant amounts of effort and production. Instead, self-selection into bureaucracies, policy goals, and peer reinforcement dominate coercion. If the supervisor in a public bureaucracy does not succeed by coercion, then what do supervisors do? Here we provide deductive evidence that supervisors in public bureaucracies achieve high degrees of compliance by selective assignment of tasks to subordinates, in which the primary advantage of a task to the subordinate stems from the perquisites related to that task. In short, supervisors wield perks, the ancillary aspects of task performance, as a primary tool in obtaining subordinate compliance.

Our premise is that bureaucratic subordinates must choose among a variety of discrete activities, tasks, and allocate effort accordingly. The idea of the task as the fundamental unit of bureaucratic organization is an old one, explicitly part of the formulation of division of labor (for example, Smith 1776/1994; Babbage 1832), or of the design of bureaucracy itself (for example, Weber 1947). Smith's pin factory, after all, is populated with people who specialize in drawing the wire, others who specialize in fastening the head of the pin, and still others who specialize in sharpening the pin. Weber's ideal bureaucracy has people who specialize in their domain of expertise. Wilson puts it well: "People matter, but organization matters also, and tasks matter most of all" (1989, 173).

The variety of tasks to allocate within a bureaucracy can be diverse. In one of our many analyses of the performance of police officers, we considered how police officers divide their time among eleven tasks (see Brehm, Gates, and Gomez 2003; Brehm and Gates, chapter 5, this volume). The vast majority of officers devoted the vast majority of their time toward only two of these tasks, mobile patrol and runs (dispatches to investigate or handle a citizen complaint). Nonetheless, all had to devote some portion of their time toward the completion of paperwork, traffic duty, and other policing tasks, and some (relatively small) fraction on personal tasks. Another example of task diversity can be found in Herbert Kaufman's account of *The Forest Ranger* (1960). Forest rangers prevent fires, seek fair prices for timber, manage old and new growth forests, provide recreational opportunities for citizens, regulate the extraction of resources from National Forest lands, maintain relations with communities, and, of course, complete paperwork. The diversity of these tasks creates the central problem of Kaufman's book, namely, given these pressures to decentralize, how is it that the Forest Service obtains a high level of competent performance from the rangers? How are their actions coordinated?

Who is responsible for allocating tasks? Some tasks are legislated. The level of discretion that an employee of the Social Security Administration has in issuing Social Security checks is next to nonexistent: Congress stipulates the formula by which all Social Security recipients are paid. Similar constraints on bureaucratic task allocation can be found in the Internal Revenue Service or the U.S. Postal Service, bureaucracies that take the form of production organizations (Wilson 1989). Production organizations are those that most closely resemble manufacturing firms, in that both outputs (work performed) and outcomes (results of outputs) are readily observable. These bureaucrats have less discretion over their allocation of time across tasks.

In other organizations, where either outputs or outcomes are not observable, the allocation of tasks is influenced by the norms of the employees, experiences, the attitudes and beliefs of the subordinates, and the decisions of bureaucratic supervisors (Brehm and Gates 1997). In this chapter, we explicitly model how a supervisor allocates tasks, holding norms, experiences and attitudes of subordinates in control.

Of course, the assignment of tasks to subordinates is not unique to bureaucracies. Supervisors in private sector organizations also face the problem of optimal assignment of subordinates to varied tasks of the organization. Supervisors in public bureaucracies, however, face a number of constraints that preclude many strategies available to those in private organizations. In a private organization, bureaucratic supervisors might be able to dismiss an employee for failure to complete certain tasks, or to reward other employees for completing them. We say *might* because there is increasing evidence that private supervisors, in facing the risk of wrongful termination suits, are more constrained than one might imagine. Supervisors in bureaucracies face civil service rules that strictly limit the supervisor's use of salaries, promotions, reprimands, and dismissals. What they may be able to distribute are perquisites: assignments that subordinates prefer because of the extrinsic aspects of the job, such as access to better computing, outdoor assignments, freedom from direct scrutiny, opportunities to work alongside favored colleagues, and so forth.

Supervisors in public bureaucracies possess few of the tools that a supervisor in a private firm might use to handle task assignment problems, or principal-agency problems in general. Civil service laws constrain, in powerful ways, the ability of supervisors to dismiss or promote, even to issue reprimands or rewards. The permanence of public unions precludes most serious, noncontractual side-payments. Public bureaucracy supervisors do not have a residual to redistribute. Regardless of how well a bureau performs, bureaucratic administrators have no economic surplus with which to devise a scheme for efficient monitoring (Moe 1984, 762). These supervisors may not even have a visible product which permits them to ascertain team productivity, much less individual productivity. The potent dynamics of self-selection into bureaucracies even limits what supervisors might do to coerce compliant production, in two directions: supervisors do not coerce those who already produce, and cannot coerce those for whom punishments fall below leisure or political gains from shirking or sabotage (Brehm and Gates 1992, 1997).

What, then, can supervisors in public bureaucracies do to encourage a more productive workforce? This chapter presents one mechanism: they can selectively assign subordinates on the basis of the appeal of the ancillary aspects of jobs, or more particularly, rely on the allocation of perks in their assignment of tasks across subordinates. Some examples may help.

The main headquarters of the Bureau of the Census in Suitland, Maryland, provides some illustrations. The facility, located in the suburbs of Washington, D.C., more closely resembles a federal penitentiary than a research center. The facility is ringed by fences topped with razor wire, is built from anonymous and gray cinderblock, and is physically isolated from the rest of the suburban community. Entry to the facility requires multiple identification checks. Yet the facility retains a good degree of cheer, is quite productive, even a desirable location for professionals who could just as well seek employment in the private sector.

There are, probably, some employees who identify with the mission of the agency. There are others whose contributions hinge on the pecuniary returns to participation. But for the talented statisticians and social scientists who continue to work for the Census Bureau despite external opportunities, one factor is surely the chance to work on interesting problems, with sophisticated computing equipment, among talented peers. These are the perquisites which census supervisors might use to gain greater productivity from subordinates.

The U.S. Forest Service is a prestigious organization but scholars have long noted the tensions to disunity (for example, Kaufman 1960), which could easily attenuate the organizational needs in favor of local constituency preferences. The Forest Service resolves these tensions to disunity through a phalanx of methods, including rapid rotation of assignments, improvements in field-to-office communication, a pile of paperwork tall enough to topple a Sequoia, but it cannot use purely coercive pecuniary measures save for those permitted under civil service regulations and union agreements. What the Forest Service can manipulate is one of the principal reasons a subordinate would enlist in the Forest Service to begin with: the opportunity to work in some of the most majestic settings our very beautiful country has to offer.

The competition among police officers for promotions to police detective is fierce, but not fully explained by simple pecuniary benefits. In a typical American municipal police force, detectives are paid somewhat more than beat police, but detectives do not have to wear the police blues, do not have to interpose themselves in domestic disputes, do not have to perform traffic duty, and do have the opportunity to be recognized by their peers and superiors for closing cases.

These are three examples of the use of perquisites for manipulation of subordinate compliance. Of course, other jobs in public bureaucracies do not lend themselves to easy manipulation of perks. An example at hand illustrates the difficulties some supervisors may have in manipulating these extrinsic aspects of the job:

Thule AFB [in Greenland] is considered one of the places where assignment is a punishment . . . one of the hard case assignments.

A C-141 was preparing for departure from Thule, and they were waiting for the truck to arrive to pump out the sewage holding tank. The aircraft commander was in a hurry, but the truck was late in arriving, and the airman was extremely slow in getting the tank pumped out.

The commander apparently berated the airman for his lack of speed and promised punishment.

The airman responded, "Sir, I have no stripes, it is 20 below zero, I am stationed in Thule and I am pumping shit out of airplanes. Just what are you planning to do to punish me?" (Richer 2000)

The Allocation Problem in General

Task allocation can be thought of as a variant of a general two-sided matching problem. The basic idea of such a game is that there are two sets of actors who have an interest in being matched with one another, such as couples in marriage, students and colleges, residents and hospitals. David Gale and Lloyd Shapely (1962), who introduced this class of game, prove that a stable matching will always exist such that all agents on opposite sides of a market who prefer to form a pair with each other can do so.

Lloyd Shapley and Martin Shubik (1971) demonstrate how this could be applied to the optimal matching of consumers and producers in all varieties of markets, from monopoly or monopsony to markets with numerous actors on both sides.[1] Many have modeled the allocation problem. A variety of approaches to these various models exist (for a review, see Roth and Sotomayor 1990). One particular application regards matching individuals to jobs, for example, residents (medical interns) and hospitals (Roth 2003). Vincent Crawford and Elsie Knoer (1981) and Alexander Kelso and Crawford (1982) generalize the Shapley and Shubik (1971) approach and apply their model to the job market.[2] Two-sided matching games have also featured the timing of matches. Ted Bergstrom and Mark Bagnoli (1993) analyze the causes of marriage delay, and Alvin Roth and Xiaolin Xing (1994) examine the early hiring in certain job markets. Nonetheless, no one has applied the concept to task allocation within an organization.

The game developed below reflects the Shapley and Shubik (1971) assignment game and the job assignment problem Crawford and Knoer (1981) developed.[3] Nonetheless, the context of a public bureaucracy prevents us from using prices (Shapley and Shubik 1971) or salaries (Crawford and Knoer 1981) in our analysis. We therefore cannot simply apply the model to a new setting, but must develop a model explicitly applicable to public bureaucracies.

Task Assignment in Public Bureaucracies

Here we develop a game to model how supervisors assign subordinates to different tasks in a public bureaucracy. More generally, we analyze how tasks are allocated in such organizations. Given that this problem is within a civil service environment where supervisors have limited discretion over salaries and there are no proper residuals to distribute as in a private sector firm, we feature the inputs of production along the

Table 4.1   Notation Summary

i = subordinate agent, $(i = 1, 2, \ldots, m)$
j = tasks, $(j = 1, 2, \ldots, n)$
w_{ij} = work input by agent i on task j
d_{ij} = desirability of task
q = perks
s_i = supervisory input

Source: Authors' compilation.

lines of the enhanced principal-agent model developed in Brehm and Gates (1994, 1997).

Assume that there are m subordinates and n tasks. We consider subordinates, $i = 1, \ldots, m$, and tasks, $j = 1, \ldots, n$. Each subordinate, i, is evaluated in terms of his[4] *work* input to perform task j, w_{ij},[5] the *desirability* of task, j, d_{ij}, the amount of *supervisory time* associated with i working on j, s_{ij}, and the *perks* associated with a particular task and distributed by the supervisor to i, q_{ij}. The specific amount of task related perks allocated to i on task, j at time, t, is designated as, $q_{ij}(t)$. Note that perks do not derive from productivity (and are not a residual). We will assume that the sum of perks are constrained ($\Sigma q_{ij} = Q$).

We make several simplifying assumptions. All of the factors—w_{ij}, d_{ij}, s_{ij}, and q_{ij}—are assumed to be integers. We also assume that each is interchangeable or transferable. Thus, we can consider $(w_{ij} + s_{ij}) - q_{ij}$ as the net productivity to the organization with respect to the subordinate's work input (w_{ij}) and the supervisor's input (s_{ij}) toward task j, reduced by the costs of the perks associated with the task (q_{ij}). Likewise, a subordinate's satisfaction with a task assignment is $(d_{ij} - w_{ij}) + q_{ij}$. Furthermore, we assume that w_{ij} and d_{ij}—the desirability of a task assignment and the amount of work spent on a task—are not affected by other subordinates. These factors are independent across is. We also rule out ties, whereby no subordinate can be indifferent between two tasks.

Thus a subordinate's satisfaction with a task is $(d_{ij} - w_{ij}) + q_{ij}$, such that satisfaction is the sum of the perks of a task plus the desirability of the task for the subordinate minus the work associated with the task. Productivity on a task is associated with the work input by the subordinate, plus the input by the supervisor, minus the perks granted to the subordinate, such that productivity is $(w_{ij} + s_{ij}) - q_{ij}$. We therefore assume that work is a cost to subordinates and a gain to supervisors. Further, we assume that there is no loss in the transfer of work from subordinate to supervisor. Indeed, we assume a complete transferability of these factors across actors and across factors. In job allocation games, this is easier to demonstrate with salaries paid in a common currency. Here we are forced to make a stronger assumption about the transferability of utilities associated with work, supervision, desirability, and perks. Featuring these factors differentiates this model of task allocation in a public bureaucracy from typical models of the firm.

Table 4.1 summarizes the notation used up to this point. Before we present the task assignment game, we offer the following two definitions.

Definition 1: An individually rational task assignment is an allocation of subordinates across tasks together with the input of supervisory time such that, if $x:\{1, \ldots, n\} \rightarrow \{1, \ldots, n\}$. As such, $x(i)$ is the task assigned by the supervisor to the ith subordinate and $x^{-1}(j) = y(j)$ is another subordinate (not i) assigned the jth task. In addition,

$$\left(d_{ix(i)} - w_{ix(i)}\right) + q_{ix(i)} \geq 0 \tag{4.1}$$

and

$$\left(w_{y(j)j} + s_{y(j)j}\right) - q_{y(j)j} \geq 0. \tag{4.2}$$

Given the condition specified in equation 4.1, the net gain from either the desirability of the task, $d_{ix(i)}$, or the perks to the subordinate i, $q_{ix(i)}$, must exceed the cost of work, $w_{ix(i)}$, for the assignment to be rational to the subordinate in the final assignment of tasks. In other words, the total desirability of the task allocation $((d_{ix(i)} - w_{ix(i)}) + q_{ix(i)})$ must be positive. Under the condition specified in equation 4.2, the net gains from work provided, $w_{y(j)j}$, over supervision costs, $s_{y(j)j}$, must be greater than the cost of the perks for task j. This can be interpreted to mean that the final subordinate task assignment with supervisory input included $((w_{y(j)j} + s_{y(j)j}) - q_{y(j)j})$ also must be positive.

Definition 2: A strict core assignment is an individually rational assignment $(x; q_{1x}(i), \ldots, q_{nx(n)})$ such that there is no combination of tasks and subordinates (i, j) and supervisory time allocation that satisfy:

$$\left(d_{ij} - w_{ij}\right) + q' \geq \left(d_{ix(i)} - w_{ix(i)}\right) + q_{ix(i)} \tag{4.3}$$

and

$$\left(w_{ij} + s_{ij}\right) - q' \geq \left(w_{y(j)j} + s_{y(j)j}\right) - q_{y(j)j} \tag{4.4}$$

If at least 4.3 or 4.4 are strictly unequal, such an assignment can be improved upon. Equation 4.3 means that some other assignment of task to subordinate $x(i)$ is more desirable (or the perks greater (q')) to i than the current assignment. Note that, by definition, $q' \neq q$. Equation 4.4 means that some other assignment of subordinate to task $y(j)$ is more productive than the current assignment. If either subordinate or supervisor gain from an alternative assignment, then the set of assignments falls outside of the strict core. These parameters serve to define the equilibria conditions for the game.

Adjusting the Allocation of Perks

Our game takes on the following form, whereby a supervisor adjusts the allocation of her own time across individuals and the assignment of individuals across tasks. The adjustment process is considered over a set of rounds.

ROUND 1: The supervisor begins by allocating perks at a level equal to the costs of supervision and gains from work, such that $q_{ij}(0) = -(w_{ij} + s_{ij})$ for all (i, j). One could consider this distribution of perks a given.

ROUND 2: A supervisor makes an initial offer of perks associated with a particular task to the subordinate best able to maximize productivity within the organization, $\max_k [(w_{kj} + s_{kj}) - q_{kj}(0)]$, within the limits of perks available for distribution. The objective is to optimally assign subordinates best able to perform across the respective tasks. Given that we do not assume one-to-one matching of subordinates to tasks, we assume that perks are distributed up to capacity allowed to a supervisor. In other words, the supervisor distributes perks up to her budget frontier.

ROUND 3: If a subordinate is given a choice of task by the supervisor, a subordinate will reject all but his favorite task (taking into account the desirability of the task, the work associated with the task, and the perks of the job). If a subordinate is not given a choice, an implicit choice is made by allocating low levels of work to the task. In an earlier work (Brehm and Gates 1997), we identify pooling and separating equilibria on type with regard to the differential between the amount of work input by a subordinate with and without supervision. Here this differential is presumed to be reflected by the value of s_{ij}, the amount of supervisory input toward a subordinate's work on a task.

Several important consequences result from this differential. As demonstrated in our other work (Brehm and Gates 1997, 205–10), when the differential between supervised work and unsupervised work is small, such as when the subordinate is unresponsive to supervision and when the subordinate produces up to the supervisor's desired levels without supervision, little supervisory time is allocated. That is, our specific prediction would be that supervisors with highly recalcitrant workforces and those with productive workforces would be less likely to spend on perks. Instead, we would expect to find a greater expenditure on perks when supervisors have workforces whose productivity can improve with supervision.

Supervisors in the task allocation game, however, will regard unresponsive subordinates to have rejected a task assignment and will assign the individual to a new task in the next round. In this way, either an explicit or an implicit rejection of a task assignment, have the same effect and are treated identically. When the differential between supervised and unsupervised work allocations is large, much more supervisory time is allocated. Consequently, we expect more circulation of tasks and more time to convergence, more resources spent on supervision, and more perks for those workforces where increased supervision actually affects work allocations by subordinates. In this manner, both supervision and perks play a role in affecting work allocation by a subordinate.

ROUND 4: All task assignments that were not rejected in previous rounds continue. If a subordinate did reject an assignment in period $t-1$, then $q_{ij}(t) = q_{ij}(t-1) + 1$; otherwise, $q_{ij}(t) = q_{ij}(t-1)$. The supervisor continues to assign subordinates to tasks and allocating associated perks.

ROUND 5: This adjustment process stops when no subordinate rejects an assignment. Each subordinate continues to work on the task that they have not rejected.

In summary, the task allocation game proceeds round by round with a supervisor assigning tasks to subordinates. Perks are also distributed in association with the assigned tasks. Subordinates are allowed to reject an assignment. Those who reject an assignment are subsequently given another task. Perks and assignments are adjusted each round until all subordinates have been assigned a task and no one has rejected their assignment. This adjustment process leads us to propose the following theorem.

THEOREM 1: *The task assignment and perk adjustment process as detailed in Rounds 1 through 5 converges in finite time to a discrete core allocation within the organization for which it is defined.*

LEMMA 1: *If a subordinate i has at least one offer of an assignment at time t, he always has at least one offer at any time t' > t.*

Proof: Given the nature of the game, this lemma is proven by definition. The description of the game's Rounds 3 and 4 provides proof of this lemma.

LEMMA 2: *After the passage of these five rounds, no subordinates will reject an assignment, every subordinate will get an assignment, and the process will stop.*

Proof: As long as a subordinate has not been assigned a task, the perks that the supervisor is allowed to allocate remain constant as in Round 4. Nonetheless, if i has no assignment, at least one other subordinate, k, must have turned down an assignment. Given that rejections by k lead to an increase in his perks by one unit as in Round 4, at least one other subordinate does not have his perk allocation change after rejecting an assignment. Eventually, k will have exhausted his ability to reject an assignment. This process will continue until all subordinates are given an assignment. The process stops in Round 5. QED

LEMMA 3: *The assignment process converges to an individually rational task allocation.*

Proof: The convergence of a subordinate's satisfaction is evident in comparing Rounds 1 and 5. Consider when total work allocation by the subordinate and the supervisor is greater than the value of perks, such that:

$(d_{ij} - w_{ij}) + q_{ij}(t^*) \geq 0$ for all (ij) where t^* is the time at which the process stops, then $q_{ij}(t^*) > q_{ij}(0)$ is evident from Rounds 1 through 5.

The convergence of productivity with respect to a task is demonstrated through a proof by contradiction. Consider $(w_{ij} + s_{ij}) - q_{ij}(t^*) \geq 0$. To show that subordinate i is assigned to task j when the assignment process converges, consider the contrary, when $(w_{ij} + s_{ij}) - q_{ij}(t^*) < 0$. If this is the case, by Round 4, the supervisor would not have made an offer of perks associated with a task assignment $(q_{ij}(t^*))$ to subordinate, i, unless $(w_{kj} + s_{kj}) - q_{ij}(t^*) < 0$ for all $k \neq i$. But since

$$\left(w_{ij} + s_{ij}\right) - q_{ij}\left(0\right) = \left(d_{ij} - w_{ij}\right) + \left(w_{ij} + s_{ij}\right)$$

$$= d_{ij} + s_{ij} \geq 0 \tag{4.5}$$

for all i and j at the start of Round 1, it follows that from Rounds 1 through 4 that task j was rejected at some time at some level of perks (q_{ij}) before t^* by every subordinate. Nevertheless, such a result is unattainable, because before t^* at least one subordinate would have been without a task allocation as evident in Lemma 1 and in the description of Round 5. In fact, by Round 3, the subordinate could not have rejected task j before t^*. QED

LEMMA 4: *The assignment and adjustment process converges to a discrete core assignment within the organization.*

Proof: By Lemma 2, we know that the assignment process converges to an equilibrium, $(\theta; s_{1\theta(1)}, \ldots, s_n\theta(n))$ and $v = \theta^{-1}$, where θ is an equilibrium allocation and θ^{-1} is a nonequilibrium, which we define as v. Now suppose the contrary, that it is not a discrete core assignment. Then, because it is an individually rational allocation, as shown in Lemma 3, a subordinate i and a task j and a perk allocation q exist such that:

$$\left(d_{ij} - w_{ij}\right) + p > \left(d_{i\theta(i)} - w_{i\theta(i)}\right) + q_{i\theta(i)} \tag{4.6}$$

and

$$\left(w_{ij} + s_{ij}\right) - p > \left(w_{v(j)j} - s_{v(j)j}\right) - q_{v(j)j} \tag{4.7}$$

For any perk allocation q that satisfies equations 4.6 and 4.7, the supervisor must have at some time assigned a subordinate to a task associated with a perk level q by Round 4. Moreover, this assignment must have been rejected, otherwise, the supervisor could not have assigned task j in a subsequent period to subordinate $v(j)$. Because subordinates will have a task assigned to someone else only if they reject it (directly or indirectly through shirking or sabotage) and will turn down an assignment only for a better one, a perk allocation must satisfy the following conditions:

$$\left(d_{i\theta(i)} - w_{i\theta(i)}\right) + q_{i\theta(i)} \geq \left(d_{ij} - w_{ij}\right) + p. \tag{4.8}$$

This, however, contradicts 4.6. QED.

As with the Crawford and Knoer (1981) job matching problem, this equilibrium is achieved through a simultaneous lowering of supervisory expectations and raising the expectations of subordinates through the distribution of perks. The more perks a supervisor has at her disposal, the closer the final task allocation and production of public policy will come to her preferred outcome.

Our task assignment game also shows an asymmetry between the supervisor and subordinates. This is due only to the structure of the game. Because we have modeled supervisors as the actors assigning tasks rather than supervisors allocating subordinates' work across tasks, the asymmetry is evident. If we had reversed the actor in charge of task allocation, the analog of Theorem 2 with subordinates allocating tasks and supervisors rejecting or accepting allocations (rather than assignments) would hold true. The asymmetry is relevant only with explication of the game and does not affect the conclusions. Moreover, as described the task allocation game as developed in this chapter more closely reflects the real world of a bureaucratic executive allocating tasks to subordinates instead of rejecting and accepting allocations decided by subordinates. Though ironic given the nature of most of our readership, university departments may better be modeled not as outlined here but with faculty members deciding on their own research topics and in many cases what courses they will teach. But as noted above, if we were to try to model task allocation in an academic department with a reversal of the role of subordinates and supervisors (e.g., department chairs and college deans), our conclusion would be the same as the one reached in the task allocation game.

We turn now to the general assignment problem as David Gale and Lloyd Shapley (1962) developed it. Does our perk adjustment and task allocation game remain valid in the sense of the general assignment problem?

THEOREM 2: *The perk adjustment and task assignment process converge to a discrete strict core allocation which is just as good if not better than any other allocation of tasks in the discrete core of a public organization.*

Proof: We start with a reminder that we have assumed away ties. Subordinates cannot be indifferent between two tasks.[6] We start by defining a subordinate who could be in a discrete core allocation of tasks and perks as q-possible. Suppose that after some time in the adjustment process, no subordinate has rejected a task assignment at some level of allocation of q when the subordinate is q-possible. We further define a subordinate who rejects a task assignment j with a perk allocation of $q(j)$ for a task assignment k with $q(k)$ as not $q(j)$-possible for task j. Thus by Round 3:

$$(d_{ik} - w_{ik}) + q(k) > (d_{ij} - w_{ij}) + q(j). \tag{4.9}$$

By Round 4, i at $q(k)$ is the best fit for task k at this level of perks. Moreover, by Rounds 1 and 4, the permitted allocations of perks can have risen to these levels only if task assignment k has been rejected at lower levels of perks, thus other subordinates are ruled out for assignment to this tasks. Therefore, if $h \neq i$,

$$(w_{ik} + s_{ik}) - q(k) > (w_{hk} + s_{hk}) - q(x), \qquad (4.10)$$

where $q(x)$ is a perk level for which subordinate h is $q(x)$-possible for task k.

Consider an allocation that assigns subordinate i to task j at a perk level of $q(x)$ and all other subordinates to tasks with perks for which they are $q(x)$-possible. From equations 4.9 and 4.10, i and the supervisor who assigned him to k both prefer the match at a perk level (k) to an $i:j$ match at $q(x)$. Thus, such an assignment allocation is not in the discrete core and i is not $q(j)$-possible for task j.

In the perk adjustment process, no task is ever rejected by a subordinate at a perk level q at which the subordinate is q-possible for the assigned task. Given that supervisors assign their favored subordinates (in terms of the subordinates' work allocation and the level of perk allocation) to certain tasks first, a supervisor will prefer the discrete core allocation of tasks to which the process converges to any other allocation in the discrete core. QED

Discussion and Conclusion

This game includes a number of stable-set solutions. Core allocation is one. This is not necessarily a prediction of behavior, but instead an indication that a stable solution exists. The implication is that not all allocations of subordinates across tasks in a public bureaucracy will be stable. Nevertheless, by proving that a stable solution exists we demonstrate that such a core allocation is not only possible but to some extent expected. In 1944, Von Neumann and Morgenstern "proposed that a stable set be viewed as a *standard of behavior*—or a *tradition, social convention, canon of orthodoxy,* or *ethical norm*—against which any contemplated outcome can be tested [emphasis added]" (cited in Shubik 1982, 161).

Every organization has a task assignment problem. Organizations exist to perform tasks that exceed individual's abilities to contribute. With myriad individuals contributing to multiple tasks, all diverging in abilities and preferences, every organization must distribute tasks among contributors. Organizations that distribute tasks to those who produce most efficiently will be more productive for the most part. Private sector organizations fear markets, and in a democracy public sector organizations must fear legislatures. Both, by virtue of the need for assignment and management of tasks, will be hierarchies.

Public bureaucracies are hierarchies, but they share only a few important characteristics with private firms. Reflex application of the theory of the firm to public bureaucracies creates residuals where none exist, frees supervisory abilities that were sharply limited, trivializes socially positive incentives for participation, and exaggerates incentives for rent extractions. Supervisors in public bureaucracies have limited and often few coercive tools. But public executives do have a gatekeeping role over the assignment of tasks to subordinates, and can, given the disconnection between performance and rewards, use ancillary aspects of the tasks to increase productivity. Given the limitations in the civil service to reward and punish as well as the inherent moral hazard problems associated with monitoring, an important function of the public executive is to give subordinates tasks they enjoy doing and can do efficiently.

What we demonstrate here is that supervisors can efficiently allocate tasks among subordinates. There are limits, of course. Some solutions lie outside the core. Consider a bureau loaded with undesirable tasks that clearly exceed the limits of supervisory time and the budget for perks. Such an organization essentially would have no perks to distribute, or the perks cannot compensate for the tasks that need to be done. In such an environment, subordinates will continue to reject such undesirable tasks and there is no way for the supervisor to compensate adequately with an investment of supervisory time or with extra perks. Such an allocation outcome would lie outside the core. This does not mean that this could not happen. It only means that this is not a stable solution. Such budgetary limitations, of course, are instrumental in most principal-agent models. Our result here highlights the important role that limited perks and limited supervisory time play. This result reflects our conclusions derived from the enhanced principal-agent model, where limits on time for supervision are a significant constraint (Brehm and Gates 1997). In fact, what the task allocation game demonstrates is that perks are critical to efficient task allocation in a public bureaucracy, where there are no profits to redistribute. Both models also reflect one another in that they attempt to capture the essential aspects of principal-agent models, while dispensing with assumptions that work well in describing the workings of a private sector firm, but simply do not pertain to the public sector. As such, time becomes the critical constraining resource in the EPA game (as opposed to residual profits in principal-agent models of the firm) and perks become the driving mechanism in the task allocation game (as opposed to wages in the job matching game).

Another implication of this analysis is that with a core allocation those subordinates who are least satisfied with tasks and least amenable to supervision (adjusting their work inputs significantly upwards in response to supervision) will receive the most perks.[7] Nevertheless, this outcome presumes that these unsatisfied bureaucrats have indeed accepted the task allocation—so they must not be completely unsatisfied. If they were, they would continue to reject an allocation and the solution would not be a core allocation.

By implication, though, the greater the desirability of the set of tasks under the authority of a supervisor, the more perks and supervisory time available for distribution to the dissatisfied bureaucrats. To some extent, this result is borne out in our empirical analysis of task allocation by bureaucrats (Brehm and Gates 1998 and chapter 5, this volume). The result demonstrated in this volume, however, may call into question the assumption that subordinates do not take into account each others' allocations.

Chapter 5

Task Allocation in Policing

IN THIS chapter, we extend our analysis of the supervisor as coordinator within a public bureaucracy, a role consistent with both principal-agency approaches and organization theory.[1] In this role the supervisor must define and allocate tasks across subordinates (Wilson 1989). Tasks define what it is that bureaucrats, and hence bureaucracies, do. The challenge for the supervisor as coordinator is to match the right subordinates with the right tasks. This requires that subordinates be given tasks they prefer. In chapter 4, we formally demonstrated that an efficient solution to the task allocation matching game is possible. There exists an equilibrium solution whereby tasks are stably allocated across subordinates. Nonetheless, demonstrating the existence of an equilibrium does not necessarily prove that such an outcome is common in the real world; indeed, a perfect match is doubtful, because a subordinate is likely to receive a bundle of tasks, some of which he prefers and some he does not. Here we empirically examine this process of matching tasks to workers. More particularly, we examines the capacity of supervisors to coordinate subordinate work across a variety of tasks.

By featuring tasks, we escape the simple working-shirking dichotomy that dominates the study of hierarchical organizations. By looking at specific tasks rather than cumulative time in working, we attain a much more nuanced understanding of what it is that public bureaucrats do. Our previous analysis of working and shirking by police officers (Brehm and Gates 1993, 1997) required that we collapse together all tasks that lead toward production, when there is obviously considerable variation in the form of those tasks. It is of considerable interest to the police supervisor to know whether her subordinate officers are devoting the majority of time to mobile dispatches at the expense of time spent on paperwork. Further, the notion of tasks as the unit of bureaucratic effort squares much more cleanly with organizational theory on routines (for example,

Steinbruner 1974), and bureaucratic politics literature (for example, Wilson 1989). Finally, by switching to an analysis of time devoted to different forms of working, we reduce the sensitivity of our results to the potential for effects of the observer upon the performance of the subordinate. That is, though the amount of time spent working probably increases when the subordinate is being observed, the amount of time allocated to any particular form of work is probably less sensitive to observation.

We expand on the working-shirking dichotomy by examining the compliance of public bureaucrats across multiple tasks, and we choose police officers as the bureaucrats to study. Data gathered in 1977 by Elinor Ostrom, Roger Parks, and Gordon Whittaker (1982) detail the specific allocation of time across different tasks by individual officers. By examining the amount of time a police officer allocates to specific tasks, we have an opportunity to evaluate both the supervisor's role in maintaining subordinate compliance and coordinating work effort. Based on our previous models of supervision, we believe that subordinate work across tasks will be a function of supervisory coercion, subordinate preferences, and the solidary attachments of subordinates (Brehm and Gates 1993, 1994, 1997). Although the findings here relate specifically to police work, we believe that they are generalizable to the behavior of bureaucrats in other contexts. In *Working, Shirking, and Sabotage,* we found strong similarities across a wide variety of bureaucrats, from police officers, to social workers, to federal civil servants.

Supervisors as Agency Coordinators

We know little about the role tasks play in organizations and we know even less about how tasks are allocated in an organization. What role do supervisors play in this allocation? In what capacity do supervisors serve as coordinators and facilitators of subordinates' work on different tasks?

The traditional principal-agent model features agents' decision to work or to shirk. In the enhanced principal-agent model (Brehm and Gates 1994, 1997), we expand the options available to subordinates to include sabotage, the act of producing negative output. In this chapter, we consider variation among the tasks available to subordinates, where the tasks vary in desirability to both the supervisor and to the subordinate. The key question is: what accounts for the amount of time that subordinates devote to each task?[2] We study the role of supervisors as coordinators by looking through the lens of our task allocation game, presented in chapter 4.

The Task Allocation Game

The task allocation game models the strategic interactions between a supervisor and subordinates to provide greater insight into the problem of supervision and compliance in a bureaucratic setting. In terms of task allocation, the game begins with a supervisor deciding which subordinates should work on what policies. Every subordinate is given several assignments to maximize the supervisor's production goals. To do so, the supervisor attempts to match the "best" person for each task. In turn, each subordinate decides how he will allocate his time across the assigned tasks. Supervisors then must determine how and whom to supervise, given limited supervisory resources and that some subordinates respond to supervision and some do not. From these equilibria generated by the game, we are able to derive the following testable propositions[3] regarding subordinate work across tasks:

- If subordinates are indifferent between tasks (forms of work) and are homogeneously responsive to supervision (across tasks), then subordinates allocate greater work to tasks which receive greater supervision.

- If subordinates are not indifferent between tasks and are homogeneously responsive to supervision, subordinates allocate time to preferred activities, (largely) independent of supervision.

- If subordinates are indifferent between tasks, but are heterogeneously responsive to supervision, subordinates allocate toward tasks for which they are more amenable to supervision.

- If subordinates are not indifferent between tasks and are heterogeneously responsive to supervision, subordinates will separate according to type. Non-responsive subordinates will allocate time to preferred activities and responsive subordinates will allocate time toward those activities for which they receive supervision.

The Imitative Model

The imitative model traces its origins to social psychological models of compliance and persuasion. Two central concepts are emphasized, social proof and consistency. Both concepts come into practice whenever a subordinate faces a request from a supervisor. In terms of consistency, the subordinate bureaucrat will ask, what have I done in the past? As for social proof, the subordinate asks, what are others like myself doing? If facing an uncertain or ambiguous situation, imitation serves as a simple and direct information shortcut.[4] These two concepts are used to model how subordinates learn to respond to supervision by imitating one another.

Several factors influence the final distribution of work allocations by subordinates after many iterations of the simulated model. The adaptation of the bureaucrats is nonlinear and contingent on four discrete sets: the available set of responses to a policy, responses at first iteration, disposition toward a policy, and connections among bureaucrats and supervisors. We also consider supervisory tolerance for noncompliance and the level of sanction he or she applies to shape subordinate performance.

The imitative model simulation offers several conclusions for understanding task assignment and the role of a supervisor as coordinator. The central finding is that the more individual subordinates look to fellow subordinates for information about how to respond to a rule, the greater the degree of conformity between subordinates. In turn, several factors influence the degree to which subordinates imitate one another, including the observability of subordinate actions, the level of uncertainty subordinates face, the frequency of contact between subordinates, the policy predispositions of subordinates (both the mean and variance), and the utility subordinates derive from working on a particular task. From these relationships, we are able to derive several propositions regarding the allocation of subordinate time across tasks:

- As the observability between subordinates increases, conformity of allocation of time across tasks increases (due to either information search, or coercion by subordinates).

- As supervisors are better able to observe subordinate activity, subordinates allocate greater time to supervisor's preferred tasks.

- Subordinates are more responsive to functional and solidary preferences than they are to supervisory coercion.

- As the number of tasks increase, uncertainty increases, and subordinates increasingly conform.

Data

The specific data come from the 1977 Police Services Study, conducted by Elinor Ostrom and her colleagues in three cities, Rochester, St. Louis, and St. Petersburg. The study combined multiple methods, including observations of police officers' behavior during their shifts. The observational data provides an excellent opportunity to test our propositions about the allocation of time across tasks. At the conclusion of each shift, the observer recorded the time officers spent on a total of eleven tasks (an italicized abbreviation or word denotes our label in subsequent graphs):

1. Time on administrative duties *(Adm)*

2. Time report writing *(Rept)*

3. Time out of car for foot patrol (not on an encounter or dispatched run) *(Foot Pat)*

4. Time on routine mobile patrol *(Mob Pat)*

5. Time at or en route to an encounter or dispatched run *(Run)*

6. Time on mobile traffic work (radar, vascar, and so on) *(Mob Traf)*

7. Time on stationary traffic work (radar, and so on) *(Stat Traf)*

8. Time on meals, other 10-7 breaks *(Meal)*

9. Time on mobile personal business *(Mob Pers)*

10. Time on stationary personal business *(Stat Pers)*

11. Time on other stationary police work (surveillance, stake out, and so on) *(Other)*

We apply two means for examining the amount of time an officer devotes to different tasks. The first of these is the ternary diagram, and is most useful when one collapses the distribution of time across tasks into three categories. Here, we consider time spent on personal business (time on meals, stationary and mobile personal business), time completing paperwork (administration, reports), and time policing (mobile and stationary traffic, runs, mobile and foot patrol, and other). The collapsing of time into three tasks corresponds nicely with a division into a police officer's principal responsibilities (policing and paperwork), plus a category denoting time not devoted to responsibilities. In our previous analysis (Brehm and Gates 1993, 1997), we facetiously referred to these as donut shops (shirking, here measured as time on personal business) and speed traps (working). In this analysis, we divide time spent working between the categories of policing (speed traps) and paperwork.

If the time on tasks is transformed into percentages of total time, and total time is constrained to sum to 1, then the data are arranged on what is known as a simplex. One could produce a three-dimensional scatterplot of the data across the three dimensions of tasks, but all of the points would fall on the triangular plane intersecting the three axes at 1.0 (figure 5.1). Instead, we focus solely on that triangular plane, displayed in figure 5.2.

The figure makes it quite clear that the majority of these officers' time is devoted to policing. The mode of the distribution is quite close to the extreme lower right corner, though there is a fair amount of dispersion throughout the lower right trident of the ternary diagram. Only five officers spent most of their time on personal business, running counter to

Figure 5.1   Simplex for Three Dimensions

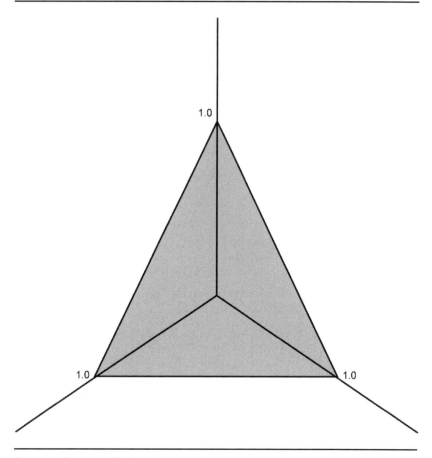

Source: Authors' compilation.

stereotypes about police behavior. Eight officers spent much of their time to paperwork, including one officer who devoted the entire shift. There are also some interesting edge conditions—officers who divided their time between either policing and paperwork, or policing and personal business.

The second graphical display (figure 5.3) involves a novel technique called the checkerboard plot. Each officer is displayed as a vertical column of rectangles (here, quite thin—nearly lines—given that we need to display more than 900 shifts). Each row of rectangles corresponds to one of the eleven tasks (for example, mobile patrol, meals). We shade each rectangle with a percentage gray to denote time the officer spent at that

Figure 5.2   Simplex of Actual Distribution of Time

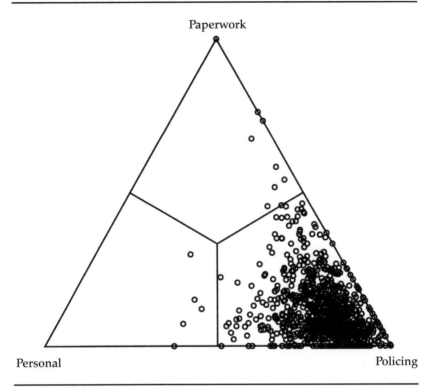

Source: Authors' compilation using 1977 police data.

task. The darker the gray, the more time devoted to the task. Rectangles that are completely white denote tasks at which an officer spent no time at the task, completely black denotes an entire shift, and gray denotes some middling fraction.

As is readily apparent from the checkerboard plot, police officers spend the majority of their day confined to two tasks: mobile patrol and on route to an encounter. They spend the least amount of their time on foot patrol, mobile traffic, and stationary traffic. Officers spend middling amounts completing reports or performing other administrative duties, as well as on meals or stationary personal business. The meals category is in third place, on average, but distantly behind runs and mobile patrol.

As is also apparent, these patterns are strikingly homogeneous across the more than 900 police officers in the three cities. Although one can identify individuals who devote significant time to administration and reports (the dark lines in those sections of the plot), as well as those who

Figure 5.3   Checkerboard Plot of Actual Distribution

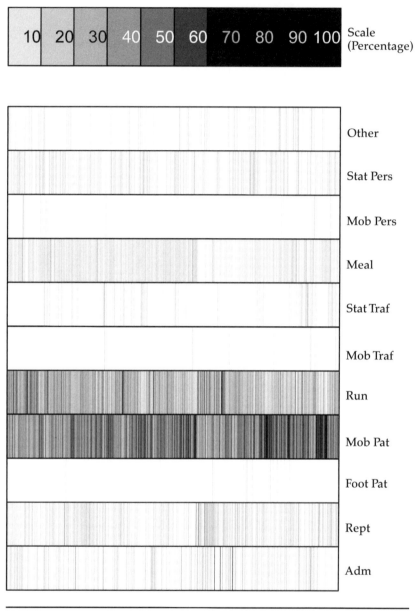

Source: Authors' compilation of 1977 police data.

engage in nearly twice as much time at meals as other officers, the general pattern here is one of uniformity, not variation.

This pattern of results is consistent with several conditions of the task allocation and imitative model. The pattern of convergence on runs or mobile patrol in all three cities could be produced under the first and third hypotheses of the task allocation model: it could be that the subordinates are either largely indifferent between tasks, or that the subordinates are fairly responsive to supervision or to the rewards offered by supervisors (that is, perks). The mean behavior is also consistent with the logic of the imitative model, which generates a high degree of conformity as a result of intersubordinate contact and high solidary preferences. In other words, the pattern of time allocations could be due to common supervision (with regard to oversight as well as rewards) or due to conformity resulting from imitation.

To test the propositions of the task allocation and imitative models, we require certain explanatory variables. First are measures for the degree of supervision supplied. Here, we use the number of contacts with the supervisor. Although we do not know how the supervisor is spending his or her time with the subordinate, the extent of contact is an excellent proxy for the time available for supervision.[5] Note that frequency of contact does not explicitly capture the duration of contact. One could reasonably suppose that the least responsive bureaucrats receive not only more frequent but also longer periods of contact with their supervisors than more responsive bureaucrats.

We also include a dummy variable for radio contact to denote how observable the officer is to the supervisor. Indeed, observability is the key issue of the moral hazard problem featured in principal-agent models. The imitative model explicitly models the supervisor's ability to observe subordinate output, though it predicts that observability is only weakly related to increased effort. We also need measures of the subordinates' preferences for work. The EPA, task allocation, and imitative models argue that subordinate preferences directly affect the time spent on work. We use subordinates' expression of functional likes or dislikes (specifically commenting in the positive or negative about the responsibilities of officers). The imitative model argues that intersubordinate contacts influence performance. We use a count of the number of contacts with fellow officers, and whether the officer expressed a solidary like or dislike.

Inferential Methods for Analysis of Time Allocation

Suppose that one has a record for each bureaucrat i of the proportion of total time that the bureaucrat spends on each task j, denoted y_{ij}. Suppose further that the list of tasks $1 \ldots J$ are mutually exclusive and exhaustive, and that minimal time is spent on each task. By definition, then, both of the following hold:

$$y_{ij} > 0, \forall_j = 1 \ldots J \tag{5.1}$$

$$\sum_{i=1}^{J} y_{ij} = 1 \tag{5.2}$$

These two features mean that the allocation of time across tasks y_{ij} constitutes a *simplex*. Mathematical features of a simplex will mean that the distributions of the y_{ij} are not independent. For example, if one knows the values of y_{i1} up through $y_{i(J-1)}$, then one knows the value of y_j. In the simplest case, let y_{i1} describe the amount of time spent working. If shirking constitutes any time not spent working, then $y_{i2} = 1 - y_{i1}$. When the number of tasks increases beyond two, the relationship is no longer as immediately straightforward—increased time at task one means less time for the remaining tasks, but not necessarily any one particular of the remaining tasks—but it is still constrained. Similar problems are evident in any situation in which a variable is characterized by multiple outcomes that sum to unity for each observation.[6] Problems in this general class are referred to as compositional data analysis (Aitchison and Shen 1980; Aitchison 1986; Katz and King 1999). We consider one main variant of compositional data analytic strategies, the Dirichlet.

One relatively simple solution begins from an assumption that each stream of tasks is produced by an independent process. Suppose y_{ij}^* represents the hours in a week that bureaucrat i devotes to task j, and that y_{ij}^* is distributed as J independent gamma random variates with shape parameters $v_1 \ldots v_J$. The probability density function for the gamma distribution is

$$y_{ij}^* = f_\gamma \left(Y_{ij}^* | v_j \right) \tag{5.3}$$

$$= y_{ij}^{v_j - 1} \frac{\exp(-y_{ij})}{\Gamma(y_j)}. \tag{5.4}$$

The mean and variance for the gamma pdf are both v_j, and when the shape parameters are integer, the distribution is also known as the Erlang distribution.

The total hours in the week is $T_i = \sum y_{ij}^*$. The proportion of time devoted to each task is then $y_{ij} = y_{ij}^* / T_i$. The proportion of time to task is distributed according to a Dirichlet distribution:[7]

$$(y_1 \ldots y_j) = f_D \left(Y_1 \ldots Y_J | v_1 \ldots v_J \right) \tag{5.5}$$

$$= \frac{\Gamma\left(\sum\limits_{k=0}^{J} v_k\right)}{\prod\limits_{k=0}^{J}\Gamma(v_k)} \prod\limits_{k=1}^{J} y_k^{v_k-1} \qquad (5.6)$$

where

$$v_j > 0, \forall_j = 1 \ldots J$$

One can reparameterize the v_j in terms of explanatory variables and coefficients with simple exponentiation:

$$v_j = \exp(X\beta_j),$$

where the effect parameters (β_j) vary by task, and the X may or may not be the same set of explanatory variables (identification for the system is accomplished through covariance restrictions, detailed below, and through functional form). If one assumes that the observations are distributed identically and independently, then the log-likelihood for the reparameterized Dirichlet is

$$\ln L(\beta|X,y) = \sum_{i=1}^{N}\left[\ln\Gamma\left(\sum_{j=1}^{J} e^{X\beta_j}\right) + \sum_{j=1}^{J} e^{X\beta_j}\ln y_j - \sum_{j=1}^{J}\ln\Gamma\left(e^{X\beta_j}\right).\right] \qquad (5.7)$$

Note that, to sustain the independence part of the IID assumptions, we assume that intersubordinate influence is entirely captured by the intersubordinate contact and solidary preference measures. This log-likelihood is easily optimized with a statistical package such as Gauss.

Several features of the Dirichlet lend themselves to some desirable properties for purposes of interpretation. The Dirichlet is a multivariate generalization of the beta distribution, which we use extensively in our analysis of the allocation of time across two tasks, working and shirking (Brehm and Gates 1997). As such, it is highly flexible and permits multiple modes and asymmetry. Further, the moments are easily found.

Let $v^* = \sum\limits_{k=1}^{J} v_k$. The mean of the time spent on task j is

$$\mu_j = \frac{v_j}{v^*}. \qquad (5.8)$$

The variance of time at task j is

$$\text{var}(y_j) = \frac{v_j\left(v^* - v_j\right)}{v^{*2}\left(v^* + 1\right)} \qquad (5.9)$$

and the covariance of time at tasks k and m is

$$\text{cov}\left(y_k, y_m\right) = \frac{-v_k v_m}{v^{*2}\left(v^* + 1\right)}. \tag{5.10}$$

That all the v_j are positive means that the covariance of time at any pair of tasks k and m is negative, or that any increase (decrease) in time at one task necessitates a decrease (increase) at time at every other task.

This property of the Dirichlet distribution is the first sign that there are hidden assumptions in the Dirichlet that may warrant another selection of distributional assumptions. Aitchison (1986) writes

> It is thus clear that every Dirichlet composition has a very strong implied independence structure and so the Dirichlet class is unlikely to be of any great use for describing compositions whose components have even weak forms of dependence. . . . This independence property, which holds for every partition of every Dirichlet composition, is again extremely strong, and unlikely to be possessed by many compositions in practice. For example, one implication of it is that each ratio x_j/x_j of two components is independent of any other ratio $_k/x_l$ formed from two other components (60).

What remains to be seen, however, is just how sensitive the analysis of composite data is to this particular "strong" IIA (independence of irrelevant alternatives) assumption. As we demonstrate, the Dirichlet estimates turn out to be quite adequate for a general prediction of the time the officers in this sample devote to the different tasks.

The irony, given our previous use of the beta distribution (Brehm and Gates 1994, 1997), is that the Dirichlet distribution, like the beta distribution, is capable of considerable variation in potential distributions of allocation of the compositions.[8] Figures 5.4 through 5.7 demonstrate simulated Dirichlet distributions for varying selections of the parameters. It is possible to generate, among other forms, Dirichlet which are uniformly dispersed (figure 5.4), unimodal and centered (figure 5.5), unimodal and off-centered (figure 5.6), or multimodal and skewed (figure 5.7).

Our selection of the Dirichlet is motivated by two distinct rationales. One is that its flexibility and relatively easy optimization (even for many equation systems) allow us to explore the task allocation problem at a high degree of disaggregation. In this sense, we choose the Dirichlet because of its tractability and its good fit to the data. The second is that the Dirichlet can be thought of as an outcome of some k gamma processes. In a separate work, we document that one can view the task allocation problem as a cooperative game where the supervisor encourages subordinates to work on the basis of the allocation of perks, represented as integer units (Brehm and Gates 1999). This stream of integer allocations would constitute a gamma process.

Figure 5.4   Simplex, $v_1 = 1, v_2 = 1, v_3 = 1$

Paperwork

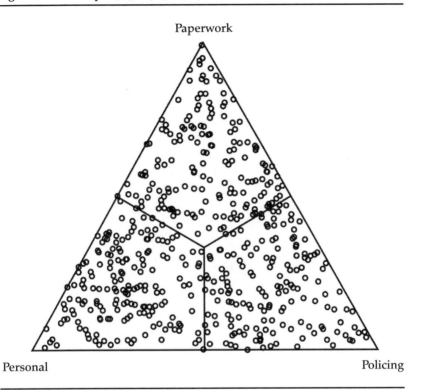

Personal   Policing

Source: Authors' compilation.

Results

Tables 5.1 and 5.2 display the maximum likelihood estimates for the Dirichlet distributions of the collapsed three category and expanded eleven category models respectively. Positive signs on the coefficients indicate that an increase in the variable corresponds to an increase in the level of work. Frankly, more nuanced direct interpretation of the coefficients across even the simpler three category model is cumbersome, and across the eleven category model even more so. A statement of effects in the compositional data setting is different from OLS (or even the beta analysis we used in our first book) in that a positive coefficient means an increase for that particular depending variable (or category), all else being equal. But we know that ceteris paribus cannot apply because all the other categories change as well. Still, one should note that most of the variables are statistically significant for most of the equations, clearly so

Figure 5.5   Simplex, $v_1 = 3.5$, $v_2 = 3.5$, $v_3 = 3.5$

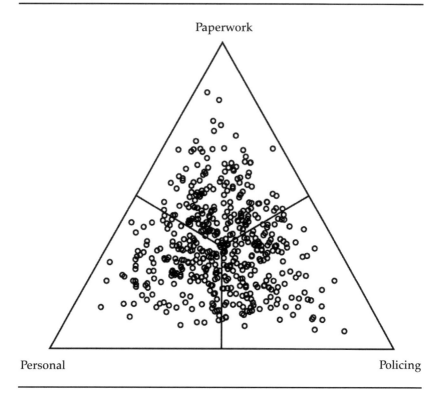

Source: Authors' compilation.

for the equations for reporting and for mobile patrol. Most of the time, the likes and dislikes are oppositely signed, which is sensible, though for the reporting equation all the likes and dislikes are positive.

Because of the difficulties of providing more qualitative interpretation of the coefficients, our principal method for displaying the results of the Dirichlet analyses of time allocation is a form of computer simulation. Although the details vary across the two methods, especially in terms of attention to covariance between tasks, the general idea is the same. The process first requires that we generate estimates of the relevant parameters for each distribution based upon our estimated coefficients and selected values for the regressors, and then generating vectors of random numbers drawn from the correct distributions with those parameters.

For the Dirichlet, the method works as follows (here, using the mean values of the regressors for illustration). First compute the parameters v_j^* for each task j from the equation

Figure 5.6   Simplex, $v_1 = 1.5$, $v_2 = 1.5$, $v_3 = 3.5$

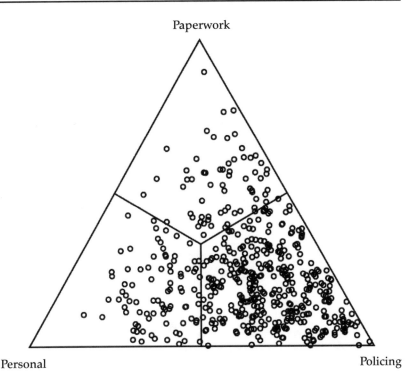

Paperwork

Personal

Policing

Source: Authors' compilation.

$$v_j^* = \exp\left(\hat{\beta}_{0j} + \hat{\beta}_{1j}\bar{x}_{1j} + \cdots + \hat{\beta}_{kj}\bar{x}_{kj}\right) \tag{5.11}$$

for each of the k regressors. Then draw 1,000 observations of y_j^* from the gamma distribution with shape parameter v_j^*. Each of the y_j^* are independent. To scale the gamma variates to the simplex, simply divide by their sum:

$$y_j = \frac{y_j^*}{\sum_{i=1}^{J} y_j^*} \tag{5.12}$$

Figure 5.8 displays a simulated draw from the Dirichlet for the parameters computed at the mean. Clearly, this simulated distribution of time allocation comes quite close to the actual distribution (figure 5.2). The mode of the simulated distribution falls approximately at the same

Figure 5.7   **Simplex, $v_1 = .25$, $v_2 = .25$, $v_3 = .25$**

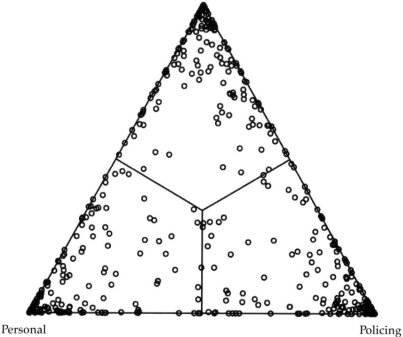

Source: Authors' compilation.

Table 5.1   **Dirichlet Estimates for Allocation of Time to Tasks (Collapsed), 1977 Police Data**

Variable	Paperwork	Policing	Personal
Constant	.51*	2.37*	.86*
Patrol contacts	.01	.02*	.02*
Supervisor contacts	.04*	−.00	−.02
Radio contact	.00	.02*	.01
Functional likes	−.22*	−.18*	.02
Functional dislikes	.03*	.09*	.02
Solidary likes	.02	.06*	.05*
Solidary dislikes	.05*	.16*	.14*

Source: Authors' compilation.
Note: N = 944.
*$p < .05$

Table 5.2 Dirichlet Estimates for Allocation of Time to Tasks (Expanded), 1977 Police Data

Variable	Adm	Stat Traf	Rept	Meal	Run	Other	Foot Pat	Mob Pat	Stat Pers	Mob Traf	Mob Pers
Constant	−0.49*	−1.06*	0.41*	−0.97*	−1.06*	−0.93*	−0.02	1.38*	−0.24*	0.87*	−0.36*
Patrol contacts	0.01	0.00	0.06*	0.00	0.04*	0.01	0.00	0.04*	0.03*	0.00	0.01
Supervisor contacts	0.02*	−0.01	0.08*	−0.01	−0.01	0.00	0.04	−0.04*	−0.07*	−0.02	−0.01
Radio contact	0.01	0.03*	0.08*	0.03	0.02	0.02	0.01	0.09*	0.10*	0.03*	0.07*
Functional likes	−0.16*	−0.07*	0.20*	0.00	0.01	−0.06*	−0.25*	−0.11*	−0.01	−0.01	0.15*
Functional dislikes	0.02	0.05*	0.13*	0.02	0.03*	0.03	0.03	0.00	−0.07*	0.01	0.12*
Solidary likes	0.01	0.00	0.07*	0.02	0.00	−0.02	0.00	0.07*	−0.01	0.02	0.04*
Solidary dislikes	0.03*	0.03	0.08*	0.05*	0.03	0.05*	−0.02	−0.05*	0.05*	−0.01	0.06*

Source: Authors' compilation.
Note: N = 944.
*$p < .05$

Figure 5.8   Simplex at Mean

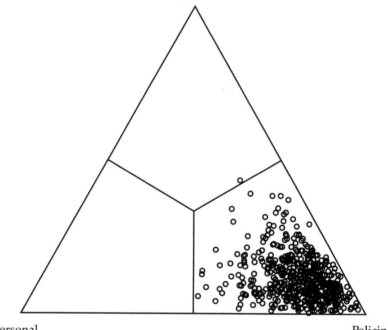

Paperwork

Personal   Policing

Source: Authors' compilation.

location as the mode of the actual distribution (that is, significantly skewed toward policing). The spread of the estimated distribution mimics the spread of the actual distribution, covering most of the lower-right trident. At the same time, the simulated distribution is missing some of the more striking features of the actual distribution. The simulated distribution does not capture the edge cases, neither the extreme outlier for time on paperwork, nor any of the cases that fall strictly between two tasks—either paperwork and policing, or policing and personal business. Nevertheless, one would have to regard the Dirichlet distribution as one that replicates the actual distribution to a high degree.

Figure 5.9 presents the checkerboard plot of the simulated Dirichlet results, evaluated at the mean. Where the ternary diagram leads one to conclude that officers spend the majority of their time policing, the checkerboard plot makes clear how officers spend their time in policing tasks.

Figure 5.9   Checkerboard Plot at Mean

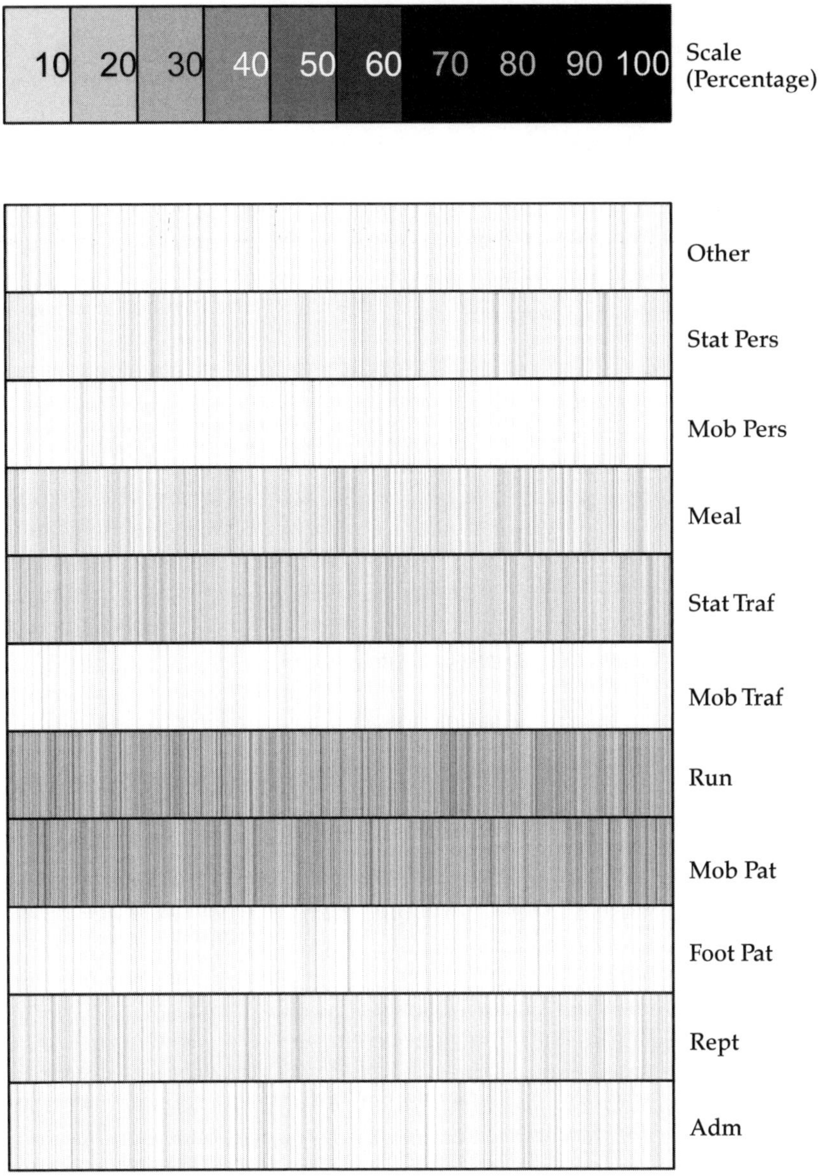

Source: Authors' compilation.

As is consistent with the actual distribution of police officers' time-at-task, the simulation based on the mean values predicts that officers will spend the vast majority of their time either on runs or on mobile patrol. Other forms of policing fall significantly behind. Unlike the actual distribution of time-at-task, the simulation based on means overpredicts the amount of time that officers spend on static traffic duty. The Dirichlet estimates slightly underpredict the time officers spend on reports or administration, though it has the correct balance between the two forms of paperwork (that is, more time on reports). The model correctly predicts the time officers spend on meals, but slightly overpredicts the time they spend on static personal business. Clearly, the Dirichlet estimates reproduce the actual distribution of time across the eleven tasks with great faithfulness.

The most interesting results will appear when we generate new simulations based on selected values of the independent variables. Although we will not be able to provide direct tests for the propositions just developed, we will be able to examine the importance of supervisor observability (a key feature of principal-agency models is the extent to which action is hidden), subordinate observability (consistent with the ideas of the imitation model), and subordinate functional and solidary preferences. In the ternary plots of the simulated Dirichlets, we will show what happens at the maximum levels of the variables in question. With the checkerboard plots, we can simulate increasing levels of the variables, moving from left to right in the graphs.

What happens when the subordinate police officers are most observable to their supervisors? This is the situation when the subordinates are in radio contact, and when they have had the most contact with the supervisor (21, in this sample). Note that we cannot ascertain the nature of the contact. This could have included specific requests for specific tasks to be completed, such as paperwork or policing, may have led to formal or informal sanctions, or could have been strictly incidental. Figure 5.10 and figure 5.14 display the simulated effect of being maximally observable.

The results of being under supervisory observation are hardly surprising. The variance of the distribution clusters away from time on personal business, suggests a significant effect of supervisors on deterring shirking. Furthermore, the distribution of working tasks shifts away from policing and toward both paperwork and stationary traffic duty. Supervisors clearly have an influence on how subordinates allocate their time across policing and administration. Furthermore, as illustrated by the checkerboard plot, the greatest effect of increased supervision is on increased time at completing reports, not at administration, and a significant reduction of the time spent on personal business, meals especially.

Figure 5.10   Simplex: Officers Most Observable to Supervisors

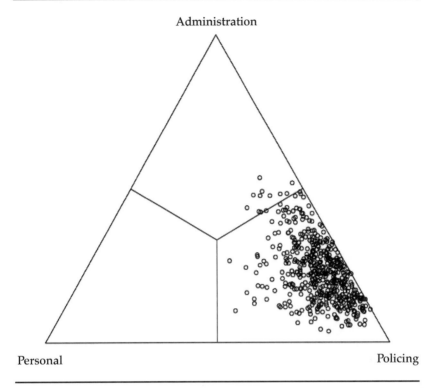

Source: Authors' compilation.

The more complicated checkerboard plot reveals that supervisors have a significant role in encouraging subordinates to distribute time over a wide variety of tasks. In contrast to the simple work-shirk split, the supervisors exercise a great degree of influence over the subordinates' choices among different forms of work.

A similar figure may be produced to display the effect of being observable to fellow subordinates (figures 5.11 and 5.15). In the present analysis, this entails raising the number of contacts with fellow officers to its maximum (31). As with the figure for officers most observable by supervisors, there is a pronounced shift toward increased time on paperwork. In fact, not only is there a greater increase in time on paperwork, but the dispersion of the distribution is also noticeably more concentrated. This concentration is especially apparent in the checkerboard plot (figure 5.15). There is an additional concentration that was somewhat obscured in the ternary plot. Subordinates who have a great deal of contact with

Figure 5.11   Simplex: Officers Most Observable to Subordinates

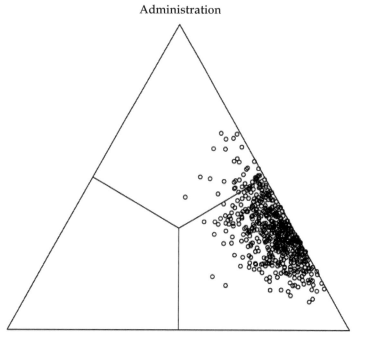

Source: Authors' compilation.

each other are much less likely to spend time on meals, which one would have to classify as a form of shirking.

Why would we see such strong effects? We think there are two classes of explanations. One follows from the imitative model: under greater subordinate observability (presuming conditions of uncertainty about appropriate time allocation), subordinates are more likely to conform in their behavior. This explanation could account for the lesser dispersion, but not the shift of the mean. The second explanation depends on a variety of the collective goods problem. Ask any bureaucrat, and he or she will tell you that the least desirable part of the job is the paperwork. The police officers' condition not only requires completing reports on each meaningful activity during the day, but that the task be completed for each pair of officers. If an officer fails to complete the report, then the task falls to the officer's partner. What we believe we are demonstrating is that greater contact with fellow subordinates encourages officers to devote greater time to completion of mutually disliked tasks.

Figure 5.12   Simplex: Officers Most Satisfied with Squad

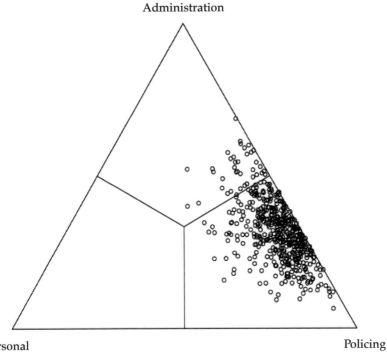

Administration

Personal   Policing

Source: Authors' compilation.

The other side of our propositions revolved around subordinate preferences. Although the present data collection permits only a modest evaluation of the effect of preferences, there is supporting evidence. During the shift, if the officer mentioned that he or she was satisfied (or unsatisfied) with the squad, we recorded a solidary like (or dislike). Similarly, if the officer mentioned that he or she was satisfied (or unsatisfied) with various functional aspects of the job (preventative checks for houses and businesses, maintaining visibility for residents, and satisfaction with the beat), we recorded a functional like (or dislike).

Figures 5.12 and 5.15 demonstrate the effect of strong solidary preferences on the allocation of work. As with the other figures, the officers spend the majority of their time on runs or mobile patrol. There is a very slight increase in the time spent on paperwork, and a very slight decrease in the time at meals. What this implies is that intersubordinate contact exercises a different effect from solidary preferences—seeing one's fellow officers frequently is quite different from developing strong positive

Figure 5.13   Simplex: Officers Most Satisfied with Job

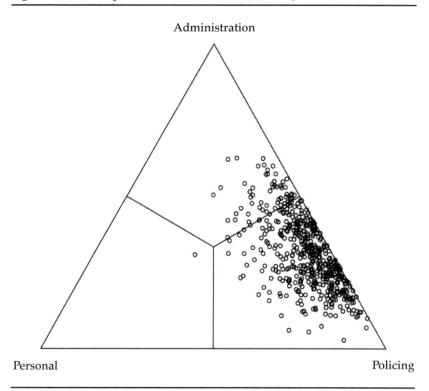

Source: Authors' compilation.

relations with them. The difference between the two plots also supports the idea that intersubordinate contact is a way for officers to resolve the collective production problem, instead of copying the behavior of those with whom one has a positive relationship.

Similarly, figures 5.12 and 5.15 display the effect on the simulated distribution of time across tasks when officers are most satisfied with their job. Like the previous three, there is a marked increase in time spent on paperwork. In this simulation, however, there is also evidence of an increase in the time on personal business: the distribution is more dispersed, and there are even two (simulated) officers who devote most of their time to personal business. There are also more officers who devote more of their time to paperwork. The checkerboard plot (figure 5.16) is the most evenly gray of all the plots, indicating a roughly equal allocation of time across many tasks. In other words, heterogeneous preferences lead to heterogeneous performance.

Figure 5.14   Checkerboard Plot: Officers Most Observable to Supervisors

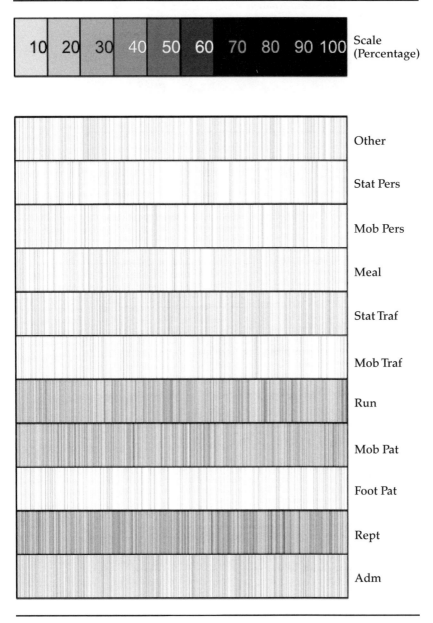

Source: Authors' compilation.

**Figure 5.15   Checkerboard Plot: Officers Most Observable
to Subordinates**

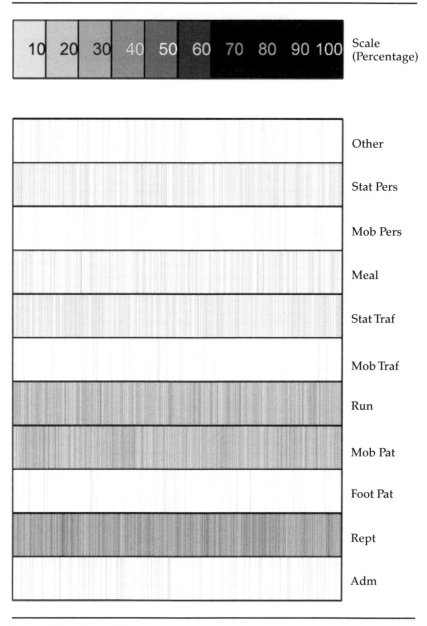

Figure 5.16   Checkerboard Plot: Officers Most Satisfied with Squad

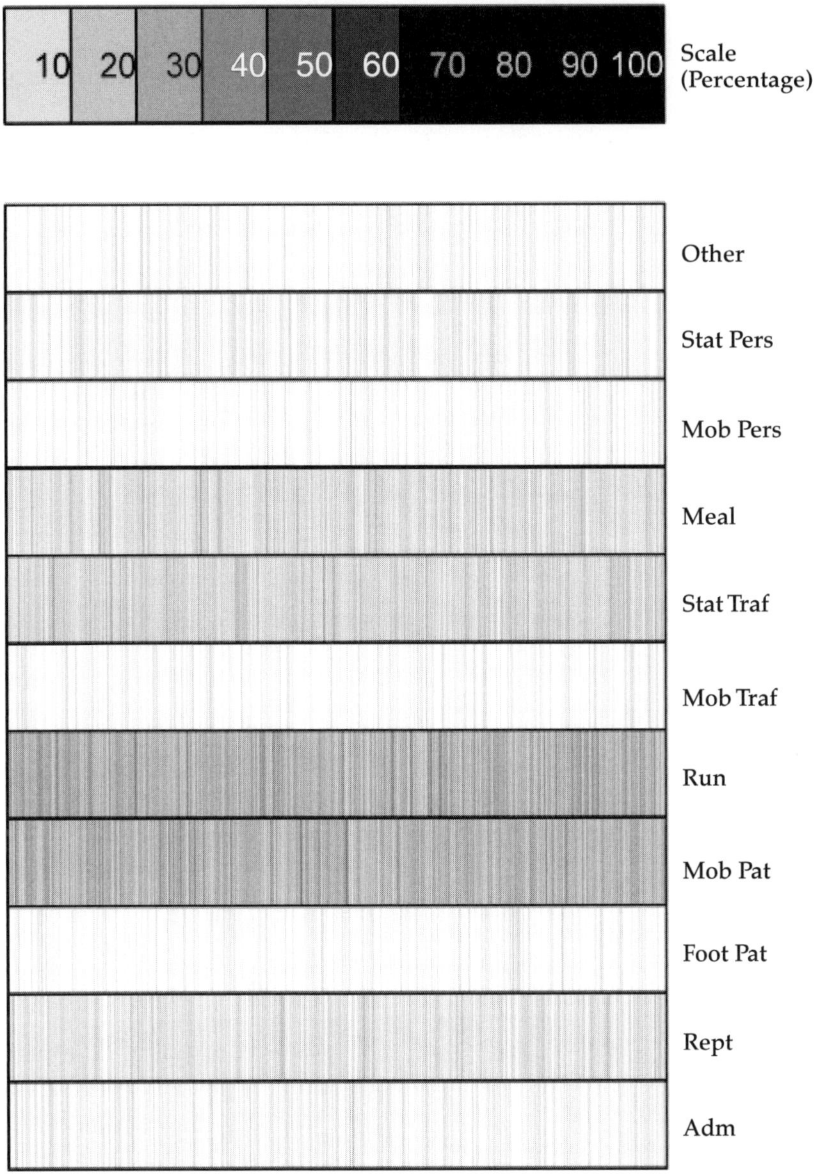

										Scale (Percentage)
10	20	30	40	50	60	70	80	90	100	

Other

Stat Pers

Mob Pers

Meal

Stat Traf

Mob Traf

Run

Mob Pat

Foot Pat

Rept

Adm

Source: Authors' compilation.

Figure 5.17   Checkerboard Plot: Officers Most Satisfied with Job

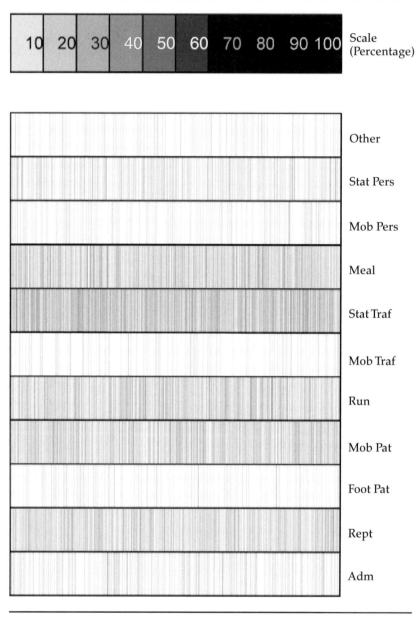

Source: Authors' compilation.

We are unable to directly test several of the propositions derived from our task allocation model. Fortunately, we are able to evaluate the fourth proposition: *If subordinates are not indifferent between tasks, and are heterogeneously responsive to supervision, subordinates will separate according to type. Nonresponsive subordinates will allocate time to preferred activities and responsive subordinates will allocate time toward those activities for which they receive supervision.* Although we do not directly test this proposition, we can surmise that police officers are not indifferent between tasks and heterogeneously responsive to supervision, as seen in figure 5.12. Although we do not find a clear differentiation in task allocation, we do when controlling for other factors.

As evident in conditions of high intersubordinate contact and high solidary preference checkerboard plots, these conditions produced a reduction to a small subset of the tasks. This pattern is consistent with officers who have relatively homogeneous preferences and responsiveness. Alternatively, both the high supervision and high functional preferences plots yielded a more diverse set of activities, especially for the high supervision plot. This is consistent with the surmise that officers have heterogeneous preferences and, especially, are heterogeneously responsive to supervision.[9]

We are much better able to evaluate the propositions derived from the imitative model. We find very strong support for the first of these propositions. *As the observability between subordinates increases, conformity of allocation of time across tasks increases (due to either information search, or coercion by subordinates).* Figures 5.11 and 5.15 show clear shifts in allocation of time by police officers when they are most observable to fellow officers.

Discussion

One of the main questions driving this book is how bureaucrats manage the inherent ambiguity affecting all organizations. Such ambiguities are evident every time a bureaucrat decides what to do (task ambiguities) and how to approach different tasks (role ambiguity). We have explored this question in this chapter by examining how subordinate police officers allocate their time across a variety of tasks. By further differentiating how officers devote their time, either across three dimensions (personal activities, administrative paperwork, or policing) or even more finely across eleven dimensions, we gain some understanding of the factors that shape subordinates' decisions as to how they spend their time and how they manage ambiguity.

Our analysis reveals that supervisory contact results in a shift in subordinate activities away from personal business and toward administrative paperwork. Contact with other subordinates results in an even more pronounced shift and a considerably more concentrated dispersion of time. Satisfaction with the other members of the police squad also leads to shifts in work toward paperwork. Those officers most satisfied with their job tend to shift more time away from policing and toward personal business and administrative duties. We find relatively strong support for propositions derived from the imitative model. Frequency of contact and solidary between subordinates play a large role in shaping subordinates' decisions.

These results demonstrate how strongly fellow officers affect police behavior. The importance of solidary norms with respect to an officer's squad further relates to this result as well, demonstrating that the imitative model offers powerful insights for understanding police bureaucracy. Our results also suggest that supervisors play an important role in shaping how police officers do their jobs.

What are the policy implications from this research? First, it indicates that there is no homogeneous solution to the problem of monitoring task allocations in public bureaucracies, if only because some bureaucracies will prefer that bureaucrats concentrate on a narrow range of tasks, whereas others would prefer that bureaucrats complete a broad repertoire of tasks. Under Wilson's typology (1989), production organizations (where both outputs and outcomes are visible) such as the Social Security Administration (in processing checks) or the postal service (in sorting mail) may have a very limited set of tasks for bureaucrats to complete. Under these conditions, the paramount problem is selection of subordinates with the right mix of functional preferences, or, distribute perks that adequately reward the bureaucrat for completing those tasks for which the bureaucrat does not have a preference.[10] By contrast, craft organizations (in which neither outputs nor outcomes are visible), such as the police force or social work agencies, may prefer that their bureaucrats complete a diverse set of tasks. Under these conditions, selection is also important, but perhaps with an emphasis on recruiting bureaucrats who, as a group, have heterogeneous preferences, to encourage separating equilibrium or in terms of the task allocation game, make it easier to make ideal matches of tasks to subordinate. Contact with the supervisor, especially for amenable subordinates, can further increase the diversity of task allocations. Restraining lateral contact with other subordinates may also be necessary to encourage production of a large number of tasks.

Because our main finding concerns subordinate preferences and observability, these characteristics can also be used to make comparisons across bureaucracies. Bureaucrats working in dispersed settings with relatively little contact with other subordinates, or with supervisors, should be expected to have more heterogeneous distributions of time allocations. A prototypical example of such a dispersed, low-connection bureaucrat is the forest ranger. As Kaufman's 1960 classic detailed, forest rangers exhibited a relatively uniform level of effort, though quite heterogeneous in how they divided that effort among such tasks as conservation, constituency relations, resource management, and (increasingly) policing. Bureaucrats who work in settings where intersubordinate contacts are high but contacts with supervisors are low should be expected to parallel the results here for the police officer. A second prototypical example is the social worker.

We also think that there is general utility for the underlying logic of our models outside of the bureaucratic setting. Learning under uncertainty is a condition that most people find themselves in most of the time. To the extent that multiple and competing demands create a range of necessary tasks for social actors, then the diversity of tasks adds to the conditions of uncertainty. Our pooling equilibrium result confirms the power of imitation and social proof in such conditions of uncertainty.

Tasks define what bureaucrats, hence bureaucracies, do. But instead of treating tasks as immutable routines or SOPs, our approach allows us to recognize the critical interactions between people, organizations, and tasks. The preferences that bureaucrats have, the degree to which they are seen by both their supervisors and fellow bureaucrats, fundamentally alter the time that officers devote to the tasks they face. In this way, the way bureaucrats deal with different tasks helps them address inherent questions of ambiguity.

PART III

TRUST BROKERING

Chapter 6

Trust Brokering

TRUST IS a central aspect of human relations, and within the context of organizations it plays a particularly strong role. Of course, just what one means by the notion of trust is decidedly unclear. One approach, quite popular with survey researchers, had been to use trust of government or of people in general as proxies for some generalized concept. Indeed, a mini-industry sprang up in the mid-1990s seeking to explain what appeared to be a cataclysmic decline in trust, particularly of governments but also to a degree of people in general.

The typical analysis of declining trust in government would examine the marginals of questions such as, Generally speaking, do you trust the government in Washington to do the right thing? Where once, in the 1960s, supermajorities of respondents answered in the affirmative, by about 1995, they answered in the negative. Robert Putnam (1995, 2000) is surely the most famous of these scholars, but there are quite a few more. The argument, they held, was that a decline in general trust in government inhibited economic exchange and political growth of social capital in its own right.[1]

Scholars affiliated with the Russell Sage Foundation—Karen Cook, Russell Hardin, and Margaret Levi among them—embarked on a series of significant studies in the 1990s to elaborate on the meaning of this concept and to identify the conditions in which trust might be more informative. Such a generalized notion of trust was to them largely vacuous: without a notion of which part of government, what the right thing might actually be, or under what conditions, the concept is a void. For example, we know that trust appeared to soar after the September 11, 2001, terrorist attacks and the valiant efforts of firefighters and police officers to rescue occupants of the World Trade Center and the Pentagon. But what were respondents thinking of when they answered the generally-speaking question? Were they thinking of the firefighters or police officers, or Mayor Giuliani, or President Bush, or the seeming unity among

Democrats and Republicans at all levels of government? Was there a sudden clarity to the meaning of the right thing at that moment, or a sudden absence of conflict?

Indeed, even the meaning of the word *trust* appears to vary considerably by nationality and language. According to Russell Hardin, French lacks a direct equivalent of the term, and both Norwegian and Egyptian lack the verb form, and in Chinese, Hebrew, and perhaps English as well there are considerable ambiguities about the meaning of the word (2002, 57–58).

So instead, the Russell Sage group offers Hardin's notion of trust as encapsulated self–interest: I trust you to do some task when I believe that you see completion of that task as in your own interest. Note what has happened here: there are an explicit self, an explicit other, and an explicit task. I may trust my neighbor to offer sound medical advice because I know that my neighbor is a thoracic surgeon (has the capacity and the will to do so).

There have been some exceptional studies of trust in this form, and these studies lend considerable insight into how people behave within organizations.

The success of hierarchical relationships between supervisors and subordinates may hinge on mutual trust, and trust also permeates professional-client relationships. Public bureaucracies, especially characterized by "street-level bureaucrats" (Lipsky 1980) exhibit aspects of both types of relationships. Consider a social work bureaucracy: the social worker and client maintain a professional-client relationship, whereas the social worker and supervisor maintain a hierarchical organizational relationship. Mutual trust in either relationship is shaped by the nature of the other; to consider one, we must consider both.

To better understand trust in a public bureaucracy, and more particularly within the context of a social work bureaucracy, we proceed with two steps. The first is to explicate a formal model of trust in a social work bureaucracy. This model, though quite simple, illustrates the heightened problem of trust in social work supervision. We then identify a series of testable propositions consistent with both the extant organizational psychology literature and the specifics of our game theoretic treatment. For our second step, we analyze a mail-back survey of social workers and case workers in the North Carolina Departments of Social Services to explore organizational trust between both the frontline social workers and their supervisors and between the social workers and their clients.

Social workers fall under an important and interesting legal doctrine that makes organizational trust a paramount condition. This doctrine, respondeat superior (let the master answer), entails that the supervisor is legally responsible for the actions of the subordinate (see Brehm and Gates 1997). At the same time, the client of the social worker is entitled to protection of his or her privacy, and thus the interactions between social worker and client fall under unusual conditions of confidentiality. Trust inherently permeates the relationship between the supervisor and subordinate as well as between the social worker and client.

Both of these relationships manifest themselves in the form of the principal-agency problem. One is situated within the organization, involving a supervisor (the principal) who contracts for work from a social worker (an agent). The other characterizes the relationship between the social worker and the client. The essence of the principal-agent problem is asymmetric information, such that the abilities and preferences of the agent are unknown (adverse selection), and the actions of the agent not entirely observable (moral hazard). The dominant approach in applying these ideas to organizational oversight is to feature observability of actions, leading to an emphasis on optimal contracts, or short of that, a coercive conception of the supervisor. Indeed, most work drawing from a principal-agent perspective tends to apply theories of the firm (for example, Holmström 1982b) to all hierarchical organizations, private or public. We argue that though the theory offers many insights for understanding such relationships, one must be careful in applying models developed for private sector firms and applying them to public bureaucracy (Brehm and Gates 1997).

Like firms, public bureaucracies are hierarchies, but the two institutions share only a few important characteristics. Important differences between the private and public sectors necessitate models of hierarchy designed with the special characteristics of public bureaucracy in mind. Unlike firms, public bureaucracies rarely have residuals to distribute, supervisory abilities in the civil service are generally sharply limited, and the public sector tends to rely on socially positive incentives for participation and recruitment (Moe 1984). These differences demonstrate that to model the role of trust in a public bureaucracy, specific characteristics of the public sector must be taken into account. One cannot simply extend the theory of the firm to public bureaucracy.

This line of research extends our interest in identifying alternative functions of the executive in public bureaucracies. The conception of the supervisor in terms of the coercive principal—meting out rewards, devising contracts, developing monitoring schemes—only weakly fits the public supervisor. Instead, we suggest that alternative roles are better conceptualizations, including that of task-coordinator (Brehm and Gates 1998, chapter 4, this volume), teacher (Brehm and Gates 1993, chapters 2 and 3, this volume), and mission-advocate (Carpenter 2001). In particular, our argument in this chapter is that supervisors gain effort from their subordinates by cultivating trust, and they cultivate trust through both training and providing political cover to protect subordinates from outside political interference. In some senses, this proposition is a perverse reversal of the principal-agency problem: the subordinate provides greater effort when certain principals stay away. In other senses, however, it is a reaffirmation of the importance of the scalar chain of supervision, this time, in terms not of moving over the supervisor's head to the chief, but of the chief not compromising his or her supervisors.

At root, there is a fundamental problem of trust between supervisors and subordinate social workers. Not only is the supervisor seriously hampered by civil service regulations, but the preferences of the agents also constrain their abilities to supervise, in the very condition where the supervisor is legally responsible for the agent's actions. There is also a critical trust relationship between the social worker and the social worker's clients. Social workers in many states are responsible for administering the state's welfare, child services, adult services, and drug and alcohol counseling. These responsibilities can lead the social worker to remove children from the home, restrain spouses from contact with the family, remove or prolong welfare subsistence checks, or certify for access to state mental health programs. This level of discretion means that the clients are often wary of the social worker's actions, creating conditions in which a trusting relationship is what prevents the more coercive aspects of the social worker's responsibilities from coming into force.

We examine the role of trust in this network of relationships between the supervisor, social worker, and client. Our central questions in this research follow: Under what conditions will the social work supervisor expand scrutiny of the actions of his or her subordinates? When do supervisors expand the scope of unmonitored activities engaged in by social workers? How do supervisors identify the trustworthiness of their subordinates? How do social workers identify the trustworthiness of their customers? What do social workers do to develop the trust of their clients? Under what conditions do clients trust the recommendations of social workers? The answers to these questions will help us draw conclusions about the role of trust in public bureaucracies.

Conceptualizing Trust

Before examining the role of trust in social worker bureaucracies, we first briefly review how trust has been conceptualized. Work on trust as applied to organizations can be categorized into two major groups, psychologically based theories and rational choice theories (for an excellent review of both, see Kramer 1999).

Bridging the two research traditions of organizational psychology and sociology with economic-based principal-agent models is a paper by David Kreps (1990) in which he presents the trust-honor game (see also Miller 1992, 2001; Gibbons 2001). This involves two players, a principal and an agent (see figure 6.1)—in our context, a boss and a worker. The game begins with the worker having to decide whether to trust a

Figure 6.1   Kreps's Trust–Honor Game

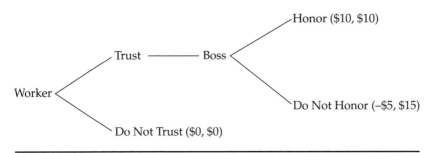

Source: Figure 4.1 in David Kreps, "Corporate Culture and Economic Theory." In *Perspectives on Positive Political Economy,* edited by James E. Alt and Kenneth A. Shepsle, copyright 1990 Cambridge University Press. Reprinted with permission of Cambridge University Press.

boss. In turn, the boss decides whether to honor the worker's trust. By honoring the worker's trust, the worker and boss earn payoffs of $10. But the boss can be tempted to abuse the worker's trust and receive a payoff of $15, which gives the worker a loss of $5. If the worker never trusts the boss they both receive nothing ($0) and the boss has no choice.

This is a variant of the prisoner's dilemma. We can solve this game by backwards induction. In a one-shot game, a boss will opt for the $15 over the $10 choosing to abuse the worker's trust. By looking forward and reasoning back, the worker will thus not trust the boss. This results in both players ending up worse off than if they had trusted and honored one another.[2]

Most interactions of this sort are not one-shot games. Under conditions of repeated play, the losses due to distrust and dishonor start to accumulate. Fortunately, the folk theorem result demonstrates that trust and honor may very well emerge as an equilibrium outcome if both players value the future and see no foreseeable end to the game. The problem with the folk theorem is that it also demonstrates that there are many more potential equilibria than the cooperative one of trust-honor. The problem is that there is no guide for choosing between outcomes from the repeated trust-honor game.

Kreps turns to the concept of organizational culture to help guide his analysis. In games with many equilibria, conventions, organizational norms, and common experiences provide the rules that allow players to distinguish one equilibrium from another. Thomas Schelling (1960) refers to these rules as focal points.[3] Game theorists have refined Schelling's theory two ways. The first approach features a series of preliminary moves in which players' actions facilitate coordination. Hans Haller and Vincent Crawford (1990), for example, focus on players' moves made early in the game so as to create a focal point on which to

Figure 6.2   Trust–Honor–Reform Game

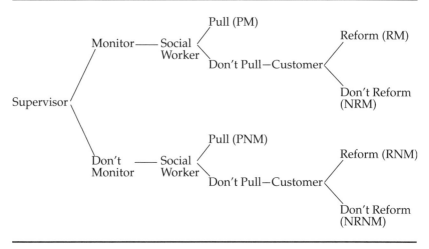

Source: Authors' compilation.

coordinate, despite common knowledge problems. A second approach features extra-game concepts such as psychological (Mehta, Starmer, and Sugden 1994; Bacharach and Bernasconi 1997), organizational, and or cultural forms (Kreps 1990; Miller 1992; O'Neill 1999) that allow coordination. It is this second approach that we adopt here.

Organizational culture provides the mechanism that identifies these focal points. "It is this psychological network of mutually reinforcing expectations that makes one perfectly feasible outcome (for example cooperation) occur instead of another perfectly feasible outcome (for example noncooperation)" (Miller 1992, 207). Trust and honor are thus by-products of an organizational culture.

Trust, Honor, and Reform: A Redux on Trust-Honor

The trust-honor game has been used in a variety of contexts to explore the relationship between a supervisor and subordinate. The game provides useful insights on organizational culture (Kreps 1990; Miller 1992, 2001) and on broader social institutions (Gibbons 2001). For our purposes, the role of trust in public bureaucracy, we expand the game to include three actors in the specific context of social work—a supervisor, a subordinate social worker, and a client.

The game begins with a supervisor who has two choices, to monitor or to not monitor the actions of the subordinate social worker. For our purposes, these actions parallel Kreps's trust, not trust choices. The social worker moves next with a choice of pulling or not pulling the case from a client. By pulling a case, we mean that the social worker has made the client ineligible for state support.[4] Given that the social worker has not pulled the case, the client can opt to either reform or not reform. By reform, we mean that the client chooses to comply with the social worker's strictures, regarding child services, adult services, or drug and alcohol counseling.

This game can yield a number of outcomes. First there are the two outcomes reflecting decisions by the social worker to pull the case, either with (PM) or without (PNM) monitoring by the supervisor. Then there are the cases in which the client reforms, with (RM) or without (RNM) monitoring (and, of course, the case has not been pulled). Finally, there are the cases in which the client does not reform, abusing the social worker's trust, with (NRM) or without (NRNM) monitoring.

To analyze this game, we will play with the relative value of these outcomes for each of the players. We start with a world in which all clients are recalcitrant and nonreform is a dominant strategy. The clients also do not want to lose the state benefits, and do not like monitoring: (NRNM > NRM > RNM > RM > PNM > PM).

The social worker wants the client to reform, but hates monitoring, and would rather pull a case than let it fail: (RNM > PNM > NRNM > RM > PM > NRM).

The supervisors find monitoring costly, but want reform and would rather pull a case than fail: (RNM > RM > PNM > PM > NRM > NM). The logic is that supervisors prefer that the client reform without monitoring, followed by reform with monitoring, followed by pull with monitoring (such that "if the case is going to be pulled, I would like to know about it"), followed by pull the case without monitoring, followed by not-reforming with monitoring ("hey, at least I tried"), followed by no reform and no monitoring.

If this game is played once as a one-shot game and a client chooses to abuse the trust of the social worker, given complete information, the social worker, not trusting the client, will choose to pull the case. Moving backwards up the game tree, the supervisor will choose to monitor. Take note, in this game, the client's decision shapes the nature of the relationship between the supervisor and subordinate social worker. In other words, the professional-client relationship between the street-level bureaucrat (the social worker) and client establishes the nature of the hierarchical relationship within the public bureaucracy. The two relationships are inherently linked in this game, which could be characterized as two-level. So, with these payoffs in a single-play game, we end up with a subgame perfect equilibrium (SPE) of {monitor; pull, pull; no reform, no reform}, which results in a PM outcome.

Note that the preferences of the supervisor and the social worker are largely the same, the key difference being the distaste, which is itself costly to the supervisor, that the social worker has for monitoring. Despite strong shared preferences between two of the three actors, the outcome of the game hinges on the preferences of the client, with the result that the single-play equilibrium is undesirable to all involved.

Now imagine another scenario, one in which the client sincerely wants to reform. We keep all the other preferences the same. Analyzing this variation, we again start with the final decision in the one-shot game setting. In this case, because the client has chosen to reform, the social worker chooses to not pull the case, and the supervisor chooses to not monitor. The equilibrium is {not monitor; not pull, not pull; reform, reform}.

Obviously, in the real world we will find some clients who refuse to change their ways, but also who are amenable to reform. The problem for the social worker is that she or he never really knows whether the client is willing to reform or recalcitrant. In such a situation, the social worker has incomplete information and must rely on his or her beliefs about the client or the population of clients regarding the propensity for reform. Similarly, because the supervisor's decision to monitor depends on the client's decision to reform, the supervisor's beliefs about the propensity to reform shape the decision to monitor. The supervisor's beliefs about the social worker's beliefs about the client's propensity to reform are also relevant, however. Equilibria in such a game of incomplete information will depend on these beliefs. They are critical to any understanding of trust in a public bureaucracy, and we must therefore take them into account. Indeed, trust is based on beliefs regarding an actor's actions and character—or. in game theoretic terms, an actor's *type*.

Recall how repeating the trust-honor game altered the characterization of the relationship between the supervisor and subordinate from one of no trust (and no honor) to one in which trust and honor were sustainable outcomes. Repeat our trust-honor-reform game indefinitely and again the folk theorem comes into effect, and our game is characterized by an infinite set of equilibria. With the uncertainty caused by incomplete information regarding the client's type, however, we can get the trust, honor, reform outcome even with a finite number of repetitions (see Kreps et al. 1992; Kreps and Wilson 1982). The other implication of repeating this game is that with each time it is played, players are able to update their beliefs, not only those about the other players but also those about the organizational-cultural factors that determine focal point equilibria. With repetition, we find the same kinds of focal points operating as in the trust-honor game. The implication is that to understand public bureaucracies, we need to understand the organizational cultures that shape the working relationships within them.

In the context of a public bureaucracy, updating beliefs can follow a number of different patterns. Experience with a single client provides information with that client's propensity for reform. Experience with a set of clients allows the social worker (and supervisor) to update beliefs about the general propensity of clients to reform. Players also update their beliefs by watching others play. Supervisors supervise a number of social workers, who, in turn, are in charge of a number of clients. By watching others like themselves, supervisors and social workers can update their beliefs.

What our game demonstrates is that, to understand trust in public bureaucracies, we need to understand the nature of beliefs, the updating of beliefs, and the conveyance of information across social workers. These beliefs, social workers' beliefs about clients and supervisors' beliefs about the clients and about the beliefs of social workers provide the entire foundation on which trust is based. In turn, these belief systems will be supported and enhanced and shaped by the organizational culture of the bureaucracy. The implication is clear, beliefs permeate organizations, constituting the organizational culture and general pattern of decision making.

Trust regularly enters the discussion of potential solutions to repeated games. In some of these games, it notes an expectation of positive reciprocation. Alternatively, "the trust associated with delegation in political institutions is, like the division of labor itself, not an explicit contract but a rule of appropriate behavior. It is sustained by socialization in the structure of rules, and rarely considered as a deliberate willful action" (March and Olsen 1989, 27).

To that end, we expect that the process of socialization into the rules of the organization should be pivotal in cultivating a sense of trust between supervisor and subordinate. The clearer the rules, the more formal processes for socialization, the fewer barriers toward acquiring the sense of trust of the supervisor in the subordinate, and vice versa. Note, however, that clarity about preferences, beliefs, and rules is not enough to ensure subordinate compliance: after all, the trust-honor-reform game outlined is a full information game, yet the single-shot equilibrium is untrusting.

There is another relationship between trust and division of labor. In any complicated hierarchy, such as social work, in which policy makers need to delegate decisions to subordinate experts, policy makers are more likely to extend trust to those experts respected by outsiders, find congruence with the values and personal styles of the policy makers, and "who leave the politics to them, who yearn neither for influence nor for martyrdom" (March and Olsen 1989, 32). As such, we argue that subordinate social workers are more likely to trust those supervisors who can provide for political cover and protect the subordinates from external influence.

Propositions

From this overview of our trust-honor-reform game, several themes emerge. Beliefs play a critical role in our study of public bureaucracy. We offer the following propositions:

- The supervisor can broker a climate of trust between the supervisor and the subordinate by providing political cover. The proposition does not arise directly out of the trust-honor-reform game, but is consistent in that one means to establish a specific culture is to reduce exposure to conflicting external cultures. It is also a variant on the idea of the scalar chain, introduced in the scientific management era of organization theory. Fayol and Gulick considered it vital that if A is the boss of B and C, and that B is the boss of D, that both A nor C should not deliver orders directly to D, instead going through B.

- The supervisor can broker a climate of trust by better explaining his or her intentions and policies. The clarity of both supervisor and subordinate beliefs should improve the likelihood of achieving trust.

- The greater the shared sense of trust, the greater discretion that the subordinate will have.

- Conditional on the subordinate's trust of the supervisor, the greater the discretion the subordinate has, the greater the effort he or she will expend on the job. In lieu of the subordinate's trust of the supervisor, however, the greater the discretion the subordinate has, the less effort he or she will expend.

Key Variables

We identify six main classes of variables to measure: trust, beliefs about clients, supervision, discretion, work, and controls. Of these, two are new to the research agenda (trust and beliefs about clients), but the remaining four had been implemented in an earlier study of Durham County Social Services (Brehm and Gates 1997, 109–29).

We define trust of the subordinate by the supervisor as delegation of risky tasks to subordinates without monitoring. By risky tasks, we mean those activities the subordinate must undertake that entail subordinate choice to provide or withhold services for clients. In other words, we want our study to focus on those social worker activities that most closely parallel exercise of the authority of the state, and hence to the game theoretic formulation outlined. These activities would include decisions about eligibility for programs, reference of clients' cases to other authorities, recommendations for commitment to medical and other outreach programs, among others.

Figure 6.3   Model of Supervisory Trust and Subordinate Effort

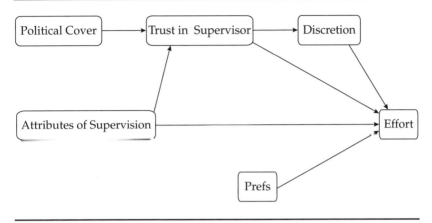

Source: Authors' compilation.

We define the subordinate's trust of the supervisor as the belief that the supervisor will support the subordinate's decisions in interactions with third parties, such as the press, supervisors at a parallel or higher level in the hierarchy, and political actors.

Implicitly, these propositions lead to the model depicted in figure 6.3. We treat *Trust in the Supervisor, Discretion,* and *Effort* as endogenous variables. We treat *Political Cover, Attributes of Supervision,* and *Subordinate Preferences* as exogenous. We will measure the positive, teaching-oriented modes of supervision as well as the coercive ones. We will measure both *Functional Preferences* (found in individuals who derive utility, such as a sense of achievement, in the job) and *Solidary Preferences* (found in individuals who derive utility, such as self-esteem, from interactions with others on the job).

Data Collection

We measure social worker and supervisor beliefs about the clients in reference to general parties, not to specific cases (to preserve the privacy of social work clients). We will develop these measures with reference to the client's willingness to reform (along the lines of the game described): that is, to actively seek employment, to participate in drug, alcohol, or other counseling, to seek shelter from abusive spouses, and so forth.

The remaining variables are derived from measures used in our study of Durham County Social Services and published in *Working, Shirking, and Sabotage* (Brehm and Gates 1997). Specifically, we will examine four: supervision, through the social workers' perceptions of the closeness of supervision, whether the supervisor administers rewards and punishments for behavior, whether promotions vary by degree of effort; work, through the social workers' allocation of time across tasks, assessments of own performance and performance of others; discretion, through social workers' assessments of autonomy in choice of tasks, assessments of the influence of relevant parties toward their allocation of time and effort, perceptions of closeness to deadlines; and controls, including demographic characteristics, time on the job, training, and promotion paths.

Results

Our first pass at the results is simply to look at the reported levels of trust in the supervisor for different levels of protection from outside pressure, and for different modes of supervision. Table 6.1 presents some of these results.

The cell entries in table 6.1 report the percentage who strongly trust their supervisor for each level of agreement with the question. For example, 40.2 percent of those who strongly agree that their supervisor protects them from the media strongly approve of that individual. The numbers are even higher for those who agree that their supervisor protects them from government (60.7 percent) and from other supervisors (40.7 percent).

Similarly, those who strongly agree that the social workers at their department learn by explicit training exercises are likely (by 32 percent) to strongly approve of the supervisor, as are those who say they have access to classes to keep up with the field. More coercive aspects of supervision yield a picture in reverse. If they say that the organization is quite hierarchical, they are much less likely to report trust in their supervisor. This is also true for feeling constantly checked—an echo of our model that assumed that subordinates hate being monitored.

Table 6.1   Strong Trust in Supervisor

Question	SD	D	N	A	SA
Protected from media?	37.5	0	18.5	21.9	40.2
Protected from government?	10.0	15.4	22.1	29.4	60.7
Protected from supervisors?	6.3	2.3	22.9	25.1	40.7
Training provided?	5.9	21.2	25.4	29.8	32.0
Classes?	14.3	10.0	25.0	26.4	34.0
Hierarchical?	38.5	32.8	34.1	22.9	12.9
Fired for mistakes?	13.0	21.8	33.8	26.0	23.5
Constantly checked?	28.6	25.1	30.3	21.1	20.0

Source: Authors' compilation from 2000 survey of North Carolina social workers.
Note: Cell entries are the percentage, conditional on level of agreement with question.

Figure 6.4   Two-Dimensional Kernel Density Plots: Trust in Supervisor Versus Protection

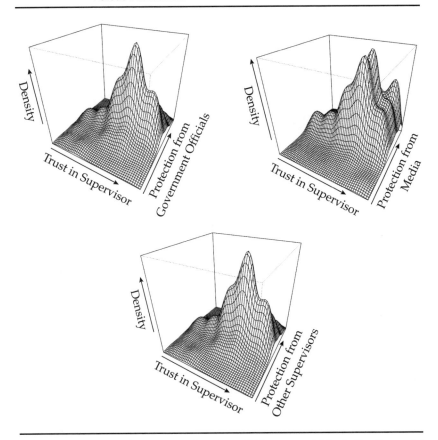

Source: Authors' compilation using data from 2000 survey of North Carolina social workers.

One can get a sharper sense of the extent to which these forms of trust covary with protection and supervision through a two-dimensional smoothing technique known as kernel density estimation. This method produces a nonparametric estimate of the joint probability density, and can be thought of as a smoothed histogram. This allows us to look at the full range of the trust and protection measures.

First, we display the two-dimensional kernel density plots for trust in the supervisor as a function of protection from outside pressure (figure 6.4). Quite plainly, the more that subordinates sense protection from government officials, the media, and other supervisors, the more they trust their supervisor: all three graphs are populated by peaks toward the high trust–high protection corner.

Figure 6.5   Two-Dimensional Kernel Density Plots: Trust in Supervisor Versus Supervision

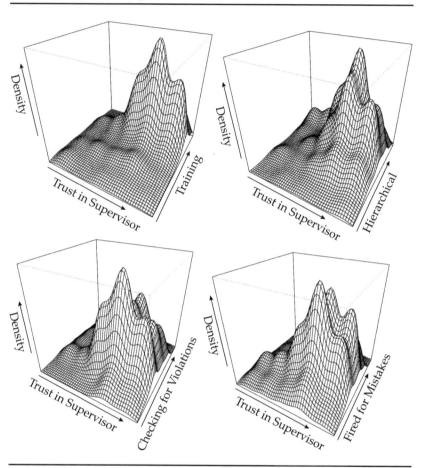

Source: Authors' compilation using data from 2000 survey of North Carolina social workers.

Next, we present the two-dimensional kernel density plots for trust in the supervisor versus selected measures of supervision. The upper two plots show the effects of teaching on trust in the supervisor: both graphs peak toward the high protection–high trust corner. The lower two plots display the effects of more coercive supervision. A sense that the department is hierarchical and that people are fired for their mistakes shifts the surface away from the high trust corner. Note, however, that, despite the differences in levels of trust, the mode is still a relative high degree of trust in the supervisor.

A finer grained analysis is possible by using scales that summarize the multiple questions in the study. We have multiple measures for each of the variables in the balloons in figure 6.3. Our approach is to use principal components analysis of each set of measures, and to select the first principal component as a scale to represent the measure. This strategy reduces the threat to inference from measurement error and provides for a more parsimonious expression of our model. The actual scales appear in table 6.3. We produce scales for *Protection, Discretion, Trust in the Supervisor, Functional Preferences,* and *Solidary Preferences.* We also include variables that refer to specific aspects of supervision so that we can assess their relative effects.

Given the subject of the essay, it is particularly worthwhile to highlight our strategy for measurement of trust in the supervisor. We continue to include a direct question: In general, how much do you trust your immediate supervisor? In addition, we want to capture ideas of trust involving a belief that the supervisor will follow through on intended decisions, acts with the interests of the subordinate in mind, and that the subordinate expresses comfort in speaking with the supervisor about problems with people in the department or with their clients. As indicated in table 6.3, the eigenvector entries (loadings) are strong, and the eigenvalues break sharply after the first factor, implying a single basic dimension.

Because all the input indicator variables for the principal components analysis are set to the same scale (0–1), we can interpret the coefficients on the scales in terms of unit changes (from minimum to maximum) of the indicators.

Working, Shirking, Sabotage, and Trust

Our first multivariate analyses of the effect of trust in the supervisor on allocations of work turns to three variables:

- *Work Hard.* People in this department generally work pretty hard.

- *Bend Rules.* If you really want to get something done around here, you have to be willing to bend the rules.

- *Hours.* Total hours worked in a given week.

The first question involves a tactic we first used in *Working, Shirking, and Sabotage* to assess the effort the social worker provides. The principal object of this oblique reference to people is the social worker, though the measure imposes a weaker social desirability component (Tourangeau, Rips, and Rasinski 2000); there is also an implicit secondary meaning to the question—namely, are others shirking.

Table 6.2   Working and Sabotage as Function of Trust in Supervisor

	Trust Supervisor	Hours	Break Rules
Work hard			
Protection	0.08**	0.08**	0.08**
Training	0.32**	0.32**	0.32**
Hierarchical	0.06	0.06	0.06
Fired	0.08*	0.08*	0.08*
Classes	0.38**	0.38**	0.38**
Too many cases	0.04	0.04	0.04
Check rules	0.03	0.03	0.03
Trial period	0.20**	0.20**	0.19**
Constant	0.05	0.05	0.05
Discretion			
Trust in supervisor	0.62**	0.62**	0.62**
Functional prefs	0.04*	0.04*	0.04*
Solidary prefs	0.05*	0.05*	0.05*
Privacy	0.04	0.04	0.04
Constant	0.41	0.41	0.41
Work			
Trust in supervisor	0.10**	13.00**	−0.17**
Discretion	−0.09**	−7.44**	0.10**
Trust in supervisor × discretion	0.19**	9.26**	−0.12**
Privacy	0.00	0.59**	0.00
Functional prefs	0.00	0.63**	0.00
Solidary prefs	0.00	0.70**	0.00
Hierarchical	0.03	2.77**	0.03
Fired	0.05	3.98**	0.05
Check rules	0.04	3.40**	−0.04
Constant	0.11	8.66	0.11

Source: Authors' compilation of 2000 survey of North Carolina social workers.
Note: Cell entries are three-stage least squares estimates for the separate structural models.
**$p < .05$, *$p < .10$. N = 509

The second question is also from *Working, Shirking, and Sabotage,* and attempts to ascertain, in an indirect way, the respondent's willingness to admit to policy sabotage in the literal sense.

The final question simply assesses the total amount of time that a subject spends on the job, in the form of a sum across tasks (paperwork, meetings with supervisor, clients, and co–workers, calls, and travel; more on this shortly).

The next stage of the analysis uses three-stage least squares to analyze the implicit system of equations. The estimates appear in table 6.2.

The models differ only in their choice of the dependent variable, hence the first two panels of coefficients will be identical.

Start with the model for trust in the supervisor. The subordinate's sense of protection from outside interference is a statistically significant and modestly strong predictor of trust. A unit change in sense of protection (that is, moving from strongly disagree to strongly agree) would correspond to an 8 percent increase in reported trust. What is particularly intriguing is that the more subordinates saw training and classes available, the much more likely they were to trust their supervisor. With both options available, they would be nearly 70 percent more trusting. The first implication is that certain institutional aspects of supervision can have a very large and positive effect. Clearly, this is one thing that supervisors, with the right tools, can use to substantially improve the working relationship.

By contrast, the more coercive tools do not carry nearly as much weight. A sense that the organization is hierarchical, that one can be fired for not doing the right things, a sense of pressure to take on cases, and a sense that the workplace checks on rules, these all have substantively small—but statistically significant—effects on trust in the supervisor. Perhaps what may be more surprising is that all of these effects are positive, where one might not have expected coercive aspects of supervision to engender much in the way of trust.

The next step in the model is to consider the effect of trust in the supervisor on discretion. The more that they report trust in the supervisor, the much more likely they are to report a sense of direction. Given the scale of the variables, only minor changes in trust of the supervisor can lead toward large changes in sense of trust. By contrast, neither functional nor solidary preferences, nor, for that matter, a sense of privacy, tends to increase the social worker's sense of discretion.

Finally, what is the effect of trust and discretion on subordinate performance? Subordinates who trust their supervisors report that they work harder, and this effect is the largest in the model. This trust has a secondary effect, because those who trust their supervisor and have a sense of discretion are more likely to report that they work hard, whereas the unconditioned effect is negative. Strong solidary and functional preferences did not affect work, contrary to our previous work. Consistent with our previous work, however, the effect of more coercive aspects of supervision is negligible but positive.

A virtually identical story can be told about the hours on the job. Respondents who report high degrees of trust in their supervisor tend to work thirteen hours more per week. A strong sense of discretion, with low trust, leads toward nine fewer hours per week. Strong discretion with high trust, on the other hand, increases work by more than seven hours.

Unlike the pattern of results for the coercive aspects of supervision on reports of working hard, there is a small and nontrivial effect of hierarchy, rules, and sensing that one could be fired for malfeasance. Combined, all of these would lead toward an additional ten hours of work per week.

As anticipated, the effect of trust and discretion works exactly the opposite for willingness to admit to need to break rules, our measure of sabotage. Trusters are less likely to break the rules, and those with strong senses of discretion are more likely to admit to the need to do so. Interestingly, functional and solidary preferences play little role as to whether a subordinate will break the rules, as do the coercive aspects of supervision. Trust and discretion are what matter most.

Discussion

What have we learned about the importance of trust in public bureaucracies? We identify three specific components.

First, our results clearly suggest that trust between supervisor and subordinate depends on the availability of opportunities for the supervisor to train the subordinate, not just at the outset, but on a continuing basis. Instead of thinking of the supervisor-subordinate relationship in adversarial terms—as principal-agency models take as their starting point—we argue that this relationship is more cooperative. But cooperation still entails uncertainty. What is the mission? What are appropriate boundaries of acceptable client behavior? What are the boundaries of my own behavior? What should I accept on the part of the supervisor's behavior? All these questions lead toward issues of trust, and our results suggest clarity and communication are the best ways to achieve such trust.

As with most work in organization theory and public administration, this idea—the cooperative bases of management—is far from new. Indeed, Chester Barnard (1938/1968) argued for a conception of management based on exchanges. One could view the exchange in narrow pecuniary terms, but Barnard clearly also considered subordinate discretion to be an aspect of subordinate authority. The notion of the importance of clarity in rules and in transactions is also not new. Charles Perrow (1986), for example, makes a number of subtle points with regard to the purposes of rules within complex organizations. Although some organizations might fancy themselves as ones in which the behavior of members is not tightly constrained by rules, Perrow suggests that they simply subject their workforces to unspoken, but still enforced rules, resulting in less morale. Indeed, James March and Herbert Simon (1958), in their encapsulation of Alvin Gouldner (1954) point to the importance of the use of general and impersonal rules in order to decrease the visibility of power relations.

Second, trust entails support, and support entails protection. A traditional principal-agency, control-oriented model of supervision in public bureaucracies has recently tended to regard the political principal as something like a patrone, the official who intervenes at every level of public service. Is the purpose of the fire alarm (McCubbins and Schwartz 1984) to have the citizen prod the higher level political official to intervene in the administration of policy? This may sometimes be necessary, but our results suggest that the ability of the supervisor to protect his or her subordinates cultivates trust in the supervisor. Furthermore, the subordinates tend to see the media, other supervisors, and politicians all in the same light. The implication is that cultivating trust within a group clearly demarcates those outside the group as the opposition, or at least the obstacle, to functional performance.

Again, perhaps the idea of strict maintenance of a chain of command with demarcated lines of authority, discretion, and autonomy has deep roots within the theory of organizations. Certainly, a key component of the bureaucratic ideal type for Weber involved the identification of spheres of authoritative capacity. Likewise, early management scholars—Fayol, Gulick, and Urwick—emphasized the importance of working within scalar chains of command and holding subordinates accountable to single supervisors. What is perhaps useful to appreciate in this context is how much this notion of cultivation of trust through protection differs from literal visions of top-down supervision.

Finally, trust is consequential: subordinates who trust their supervisor behave in fundamentally different ways from those who do not. Trust leads toward a greater sense of discretion. Discretion on its own may raise the risk of greater shirking, but discretion accompanied by a sense of trust of the supervisor leads toward a higher rate of effort. Trust matters.

Table 6.3   First Principal Component Scale Construction

Discretion

For the most part, I am in charge of deciding when to complete the paperwork for my clients' cases	.37
Employees are expected to follow orders without questioning	−.08
My supervisor allows me to make what I think is the best decision	.52
I don't feel that I have as much control over my cases as I would like	.35
My supervisor micromanages everything I do	−.43
The administration accepts the decisions that I make	.52

First two eigenvalues are 1.89, 1.12

(continued)

Table 6.3   *Continued*

Functional Preferences

This job provides me with a sense of accomplishment	.56
The most rewarding part of this job is that it really makes a difference	.58
It is encouraging to see the high level of idealism that is maintained by people in this field	.41
A person enters this profession because he or she likes the work	.42

First two eigenvalues are 1.86, .88

Solidary Preferences

My co-workers take responsibility for their actions when things go wrong	.43
I feel comfortable in confiding with co-workers about any problems I have on the job	.41
My co-workers don't care if they create extra work for other people	.22
Working hard on my job leads to gaining respect from co-workers	.35
The environment of the department is one in which co-workers help each other out	.44
The department is really very impersonal	.25
A person gets the chance to develop good friends here	.40
My co-workers take credit for things that I have done	.27

First two eigenvalues are 2.67, 1.21

Protection

My supervisor does a good job of keeping members of the media from nosing around in department matters	.54
My supervisor protects me from government officials from outside this department	.65
My supervisor protects me when other supervisors ask me to do things which take away from my main role here	.54

First two eigenvalues are 1.59, .84

Trust in Supervisor

In general, how much do you trust your immediate supervisor?	.56
When my supervisor tells me about a decision he or she intends to make, he or she follows through	.52
I feel that my supervisor generally has my interests in mind when he or she makes a decision	.55
If I have a problem with someone in the department, I feel comfortable in asking my supervisor for help	.16
If I have a problem concerning a client, I talk with my supervisor before speaking with anyone else	.30

First two eigenvalues are 2.10, 1.02

Source: Authors' compilation from 2000 survey of North Carolina social workers.

Chapter 7

Rules, Trust, and the Allocation of Time

I N THIS chapter, we aim to synthesize the extensive literature in social psychology and organization theory on supervision and leadership. We take as our point of departure an argument from organization theory: the fundamental problem for public bureaucracies is ambiguity, and the fundamental function of the public executive is the resolution of that ambiguity.

Until this point, we have been considering each of these proposed functions of the public executive—training, time allocation, and brokering trust—as separate dimensions. Here we propose that the three functions of supervision are interactive. As we explained in chapter 6, one purpose of training is to make the boundaries of acceptable behavior clear to the subordinates, and thereby to broker trust between supervisors and subordinates. We now explore the connection between trust and task allocation: do trusted supervisors have more latitude in the allocation of tasks for subordinates?

We think there is considerable merit in consolidating the three components. For one, the evidence of the effects of each of these three dimensions is present, but decidedly small. In the computer simulations of the adaptive preferences model, we found that the principal yielded small gains in the agent's productivity, even as the agent herself gained substantially in her own utility. This, we believed, was an echo of the findings from the human relations school (Mayo 1945; Roethlisberger and Dixon 1939), which likewise noted little substantial and consistent gains in productivity from catering to the interests and needs of subordinates. More recent data, however, suggest that some of the ambiguity about the happy-productive worker hypothesis has mostly to do with the absence of good empirical support for different measurements of happiness (Cropanzano and Wright 2001). There is also strong evidence to identify that when subordinates have a sense that they contribute to the determination of the organizational mission, they are more productive. In a field experiment, Edward Deci, James Connell, and Richard Ryan (1989) observe that subordinates who participate in organizational decisions are more likely to express trust in the corporation rather than those who do not.

In our formal model of task allocation, we observed that it was possible (in the context of our cooperative game) to identify a core, or cooperative equilibrium, through the supervisor's allocation of nonbudgetary rewards such as the perquisites of office. We did, however, query whether perks fell into a different kind of budget, and whether the least desirable tasks would become too expensive to achieve an allocation of tasks within the core. In the data analysis of task allocation among police officers, we found that supervisors did have a capacity to encourage the subordinate officers to devote more time to one noxious activity, paperwork, but that the stronger effects came from cross-subordinate influences and functional preferences.

In the complete information noncooperative game outlining the potential difficulties for simultaneous trust among social work subordinates, supervisors, and clientele, we observed the potential for myriad equilibria, including decidedly nonfunctional ones. Our analysis of the effects of trust brokering on social worker's assessments of performance, reports of total time on the job, and of cheating on forms (a form of sabotage) demonstrated strong, though limited, effects for trust.

In short, we have found that rules, routines, task allocation, and trust brokering are all positive functions of the public executive, but that when taken separately, their effects are somewhat limited. One of our explicit goals in this chapter is to document why it is that these functions should be seen as interactive.

Organizational Ambiguity

The literature of organization theory is replete with discussion about the functions of rules and routines within organizations. Rules and routines (and the training designed to familiarize workers with them) serve to reduce inherent ambiguity of organization. This ambiguity reduction is also clearly relevant to both the task allocation and trust brokering functions, in an integral way.

Herbert Simon (1945) identified a key form of ambiguity in public service organizations: appropriate design of division of labor. Whereas the scientific management scholars—Frederick Taylor, but especially Luther Gulick—emphasized principles of organizational design, Simon's famous essay "The Proverbs of Administration" admonished that these principles were internally contradictory and of little binding guidance.

Instead, he emphasized that organizations—explicitly, a public health organization—could sensibly structure its division of labor by clientele, task, or geography.

Indeed, one of our core examples in this book, the provision of social work services, is often organized by all three modes. The state of North Carolina delegates the design of social services provision down to each county in the state, with the result that some of the departments of social services in the state are organized by clientele (child services or adult services), some by task (welfare or mental health) and some by geography. Without an inevitable structure to social services provision, there is a basic ambiguity in the organizational design.

James March extended these ideas about the ambiguity of organization to note its many other forms (1978). For one, there is a basic ambiguity in the priority of tasks within public service organizations. Consider another of our core examples, the tasks of the typical police department, specifically the regulation of mobile patrols. Driving a patrol car in a neighborhood may serve an important deterrence function by making the police officers more visible to potential criminals. Driving a patrol car might also be a way for police officers to avoid more confrontational (and hence dangerous) interactions with the public. Even the proverbial cop in the donut shop deters crime in that particular place.

We noted a series of more than eleven specific tasks for the police officers and six for the social workers. As is quite typical among public bureaucrats, completing burdensome paperwork is one of their chief complaints. At the same time, it is also their best protection against claims by either the public or supervisors of shirking or sabotage. Tasks in general, and more particularly, deciding which one takes priority, constitute another mode of ambiguity in organizations.

Yet another critical form is in authority relationships. March and Simon (1958) reformulate Alvin Gouldner's machine model of bureaucracy such that the central dilemma is the obtrusiveness of rules and the visibility of power relations. As rules become more visible, employees become less aware of power relations. Indeed, Charles Perrow's (1986) discussion emphasizes the importance of a rule as a definition of boundaries, and also as a scapegoat for the absence of maneuverability on the part of the bureaucrat.

Training, explicitly in the form of instantiating and clarifying rules, helps resolve all three forms of ambiguity. Following Karl Weick, one might consider such ambiguities to be resolvable (in the sense of coming to some particular enactment) without being solvable (in the sense of eliminating the ambiguity). Rules are just such an enactment. But where learning by doing can make discovery of the boundaries set by the rules of an organization to be painful and not conducive to productive relationships between principals and agents, learning as a result of training can make the rules obvious and visible. Although a particular division of labor may not be the necessary division of labor, training by rules makes clear who is responsible for what tasks at what times. In a study of insurance managers' assessment of the importance of various management tasks across seven different countries, Roya Ayman and her colleagues (1994) find that there is considerable consensus about what dominates: recruiting, training, and performance management. Indeed, Ayman also suggests that the pattern of importance is so strong and consistent that it is likely that his respondents have schema—implicit leadership models—that rank these tasks.

Further, training is essential to the production of routines within organizations. The idea of routines (or programs, procedures, tasks, and SOPs, as they are variously termed in the literature) as the basic unit of organizational performance has a long tradition (Simon 1945; March and Simon 1958; Steinbruner 1974; Allison 1971; Lindblom 1959). Routines can, in particular, be a means for resolving organizational ambiguities because "that's the way things are done around here." One can and perhaps generally does think of routines as producing reliability and perhaps rigidity, but March and Olsen suggest that they have broader usefulness:

> The ubiquity of routines often makes political institutions appear to be bureaucratic, rigid, insensitive, or stupid. The simplification provided by rules is clearly imperfect, and the imperfection is often manifest, especially after the fact. But some of the major capabilities of modern institutions come from their effectiveness in substituting rule-bound behavior for individually autonomous behavior. Routines make it possible to coordinate many simultaneous activities in a way that makes them mutually consistent. Routines help avoid conflicts; they provide codes of meaning that facilitate interpretation of ambiguous worlds; they constrain bargaining within comprehensible terms and enforce agreements; they help mitigate the unpredictability created by open structures and garbage can processes by regulating the access of participants, problems, and solutions to choice opportunities. Routines embody collective and individual identities, interests, values, and worldviews, thus constraining the allocation of attention, standards of evaluation, priorities, perceptions, and resources (1989, 24).

In the way that routines help organizations and their members practice in reliable and consistent ways, routines also help to build trust by establishing reputations. One can see the problem of trust in a purely instrumental way: X trusts Y to do Z because of X's beliefs in Y's interests, competence, and reliability (Hardin 2002). Or one can view trust, as do March and Olsen, as a matter of coming to share values. This latter kind of trust complements the former.

Policy makers seek competence among experts, but competence alone is unlikely to be enough. Expertise needs to be reliable, not in the sense of having a distribution of values and styles among competent experts that encourages a pairing of competent specialists with policy makers who trust them (Beneveniste 1972; March and Olsen 1989, 32).

Indeed, the psychology literature on management is rather clear about the mechanisms for the production of trust: trust emerges from sustained and systematic interactions between the subordinate and the supervisor, and is a generalization of contextual performance more than task performance. Jerry Fuller and Kim Hestler (2001), in a survey of members of a large steelworkers union, find that interactional justice (a sense of honesty) more than procedural justice (due process) positively influences evaluations of integrity and benevolence, essential ingredients of trust. Roger Mayer and James Davis (1999), in a panel survey of employees and supervisors in a plastics firm, find that accuracy has a strong effect on benevolence; that instrumentality strongly affects ability, benevolence, and integrity; and that integrity has the strongest effect on trust.

Here we test an interrelation of rules, routines, trust brokering, and task allocation. Trust emerges because supervisors are able to establish that supervisors and subordinates share the same values, and that (with respect to political outsiders) it is a matter of us versus them. Political cover instantiates this trust. Further, those supervisors who are able to cultivate the trust of their subordinates are better able to control the flow of tasks within the organization.

What we will not tackle here is a relatively recent and largely unsubstantiated speculation in the literature that differentiates between transactional and transformational leadership (Bass 1985; see also Bycio, Hackett, and Allen 1997). Transactional leaders manage the exchange of remunerations for tasks, whereas transformational leaders exercise a charismatic leadership that stimulates and leads toward a shared sense of valued outcomes. Not only is the literature largely untested, but the present circumstances of the highly constrained bureaucratic supervisor make it impossible for us to do so here.

Time to Task

Our data analytic strategy will look at the subordinate's time-to-task as the ultimate dependent variable. As in our earlier chapters, the advantages of focusing on task allocation are multiple. Although the social desirability (aka Hawthorne) effects may both suppress shirking while under observation and discourage faithful reports of levels of work, the task allocation problem looks within categories of work. That is, by changing our question, from how much work to how much at which kinds of work, we may evade some of the obvious limits on self-reported data.

In this study, we asked social workers to summarize the time they would spend in six tasks: completing paperwork, meeting with their supervisor, meeting with clients, meeting with co-workers, making calls, and traveling to appointments. In figure 7.1, we display the kernel density plots of the distribution of the amount of time the subordinates spent on these facets of their jobs.

As is immediately apparent from the kernel density plots, two tasks tend to dominate the typical social worker's workweek: time spent completing paperwork, and time with clients. That these two tasks tend to dominate the social worker's time is hardly a surprise, given that working with the clients is their principal task, and documenting their decisions is of paramount importance. The kernel density plots for these two tasks also reveal that some social workers may spend as much as forty hours, and that the distribution is skewed toward the larger end.

The modes for the remaining tasks (meeting with the supervisor or co-workers, time on calls, and time traveling) are all at about three hours per week, but some social workers spend the preponderance of their time on these tasks.

The checkerboard plot in figure 7.2 is quite revealing of the typical social worker's day. The two darkest horizontal stripes are clearly those for time with clients and time on paperwork, consistent with the univariate kernel density plots. If one follows a vertical column, it is clear that those social workers who spend a lot of time at either task (a cell is especially dark) spend less time on the other, but still more time on that alternate task than on any other. One can also see that those who spend roughly equal time on the two tasks also spend very little time on the other tasks.

It is noteworthy that the time spent with the supervisor is nearly uniformly low. The entire row is white to light gray, consistent with a mode of three hours per week. Is this because supervision is effective in North Carolina social services? The pattern would seem to indicate that social workers spend most of their time on the central tasks of their profession, with relatively little supervisory intervention. Alternatively, is this pattern the result of the constraints that tasks impose on subordinates? Perhaps the uniform patterns indicate simply that the social workers have little discretion in how they allocate their time.

There are some exceptions in the sample. A handful of social workers spend the preponderance of their time traveling: note the few very black bars in the top row. One would anticipate that these individuals would have duties that would take them into far-flung areas of the state. Although a few spend the preponderance of their time with co-workers, the proportion is not as striking as the time on travel.

Figure 7.1   Kernel Density Plots of Time on Tasks

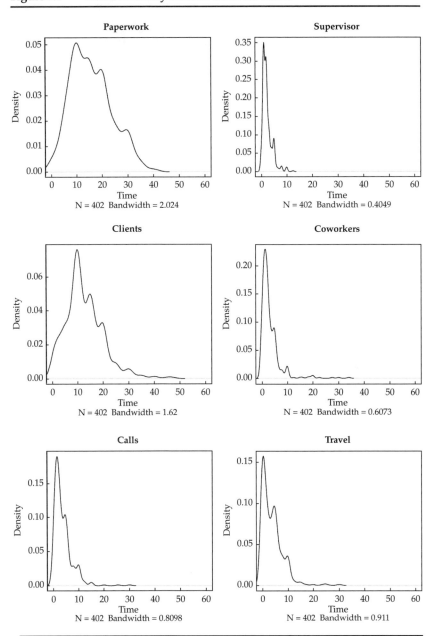

Source: Authors' compilation using data from 2000 survey of North Carolina social workers.

Figure 7.2   Checkerboard Plot: Task Allocation Among Social Workers

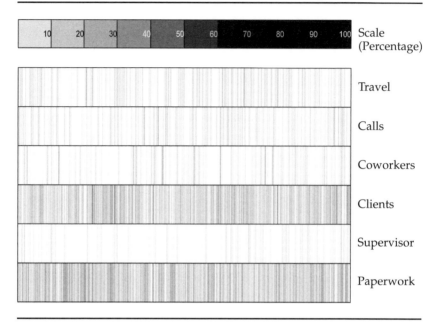

Source: Authors' compilation using data from 2000 survey of North Carolina social workers.

We again rely on the Dirichlet to analyze these compositional data. Table 7.1 documents the first differences for the change in time to task after a shift from the mean to the observed maximum for each variable, holding all other variables at their means. These first difference values serve as measures of the estimated effects of each variable on the allocation of time on different tasks. These values appear in the bottom portion of the table. Coefficient values appear in the upper part and those significant at $p < 0.05$ are designated. The first point to draw from the estimated effects is that despite the patterns of statistical significance, the actual shifts in time per task are relatively small and constrained. Very few of the variables would account for more than a 10 percent change in the time to any particular task. One could take this result to read that subordinates are significantly constrained in their discretion about time to task, and that supervisors do not exercise a great influence in shifting time to task.

The effect of trust in the supervisor on time to task is small for all of the specific tasks. Subordinates who express a high degree of trust in their supervisors may decrease time to paperwork by about 5 percent per week and increase time spent with supervisor and co-workers by about 2 percent. This result is consistent with a story that subordinates

Table 7.1 Dirichlet Maximum Likelihood: Time Allocation by Social Workers

	Paperwork	Supervisor	Clients	Co-Workers	Calls	Travel
Coefficients						
Trust in supervisor	-.24*	.36*	.03	-.24*	.15	.22*
Discretion	.04*	-.02	-.01	.05*	.05	-.01
Trust × discretion	.08*	-.05*	.03*	-.04*	-.01	.01
Functional preferences	-.05*	-.01	.02	-.00	.03	.01
Solidary preferences	-.06	-.00	.06*	.00	.02	-.04
Protection	.00	.04	.10*	.00	-.03	.06*
Privacy	.00	.00	-.05*	-.01	-.07*	-.07*
Hierarchical?	-.01	.10	.23	-.08	-.20*	-.49
Fired?	.09	.29*	-.19*	-.51*	-.18*	-.03
Check for rules?	.04	.07	-.25	.08	-.02	-.15*
Constant	1.63	-.22	1.20	.11	.08	-.15
Estimated Effects						
Trust in supervisor	-.40	.03	.33	-.16	-.05	.151
Discretion	.01	-.11	-.10	.09	.12	.01
Trust × discretion	.58	-.31	.28	-.16	-.28	-.10
Functional preferences	-.30	-.07	.09	.10	.08	.11
Solidary preferences	-.35	-.31	.33	.11	.32	-.28
Protection	-.34	-.10	.14	-.10	-.10	.03
Privacy	-.26	-.10	-.21	.26	.10	.01
Hierarchical?	.07	.10	.14	-.07	-.13	-.12
Fired?	.30	.27	-.14	-.34	-.27	.18
Check for rules?	.09	.07	-.14	-.09	-.07	.11

Source: Authors' compilation from 2000 survey of North Carolina social workers.

Note: Coefficients report estimates for the Dirichlet distribution estimated with maximum likelihood. Estimated effects report the estimated change in time devoted to that task given a change from the mean to the observed maximum, holding all other variables at the mean.

$*p < .05$, N = 509

spend significant amounts of time completing their paperwork when they have difficulty trusting their supervisor, and hence need to justify their actions more. But that story would not be consistent with the effect of discretion on paperwork. Surprisingly, those social workers who express a great sense of discretion spend 14 percent more time on paperwork, despite the near universal distaste for the task. In fact, discretion leads to less time spent on every other task, some of which one would assume would be more preferred.

The combination of high trust and a sense of discretion, however, obliterates the effect of trust and discretion on their own and nearly completely wipes out the independent effects of each on all the categories of tasks. Note in particular the effect on paperwork—a reduction, in great contrast to the effect of discretion alone.

Both functional and solidary preferences play a major role in reshaping the time that subordinates devote to particular tasks. Those with strong functional preferences tend to reduce their time on paperwork, apparently shifting it to clients in equal proportion. Subordinates with strong solidary preferences would also cut back, but also on clients, spending that time with co-workers, the supervisor, and on calls.

Quite significantly, the social worker who feels that his or her supervisor protects him or her from outside interference (other supervisors, government officials, and the media), would see less time spent on paperwork, and quite a bit more with clients. The argument that the supervisor's role is to broker trust and to shield the agent from the "fire alarm" is apparently quite functional.

The effect of the more coercive aspects of supervision is somewhat mixed. Respondents who thought their department was hierarchical would spend 6 percent less on paperwork, and those who believed both that one could be fired for rule violations and that those rules were constantly being checked would significantly increase time to paperwork. Fear of being fired also was associated with a 4 percent reduction in time spent with co-workers, though the result was not statistically significant.

We can see more into the tradeoffs between the different tasks with simulations coupled with the checkerboard plot (figure 7.3). In the upper left, we display the effect of a shift in trust in the supervisor from the least to the most. The stripe for paperwork moves from the dominant fraction of the social worker's time to the minimum, whereas time with co-workers, clients, and the supervisor clearly increases.

In the upper right, we see an even more pronounced version of a similar pattern due to increasing sense of discretion: time to paperwork significantly declines, whereas time on calls and with co-workers, clients, and supervisors all increase.

In the bottom panels, we see that the effect of functional preferences somewhat increases time with clients, but decreases time on calls, with

Figure 7.3   Checkerboard Plots: Time on Tasks

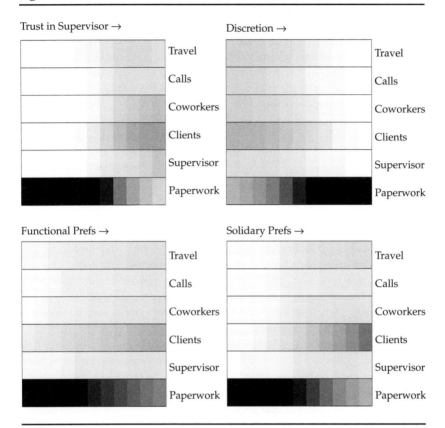

Trust in Supervisor →

	Travel
	Calls
	Coworkers
	Clients
	Supervisor
	Paperwork

Discretion →

	Travel
	Calls
	Coworkers
	Clients
	Supervisor
	Paperwork

Functional Prefs →

	Travel
	Calls
	Coworkers
	Clients
	Supervisor
	Paperwork

Solidary Prefs →

	Travel
	Calls
	Coworkers
	Clients
	Supervisor
	Paperwork

Source: Authors' compilation using data from 2000 survey of North Carolina social workers.

co-workers, with supervisors, and on paperwork. The effect of increased solidary preferences increases time with co-workers, apparently at the expense of time on calls and results in a slight decrease in time devoted to paperwork. These simulations provide a dynamic perspective of the relationship between these aspects of a social worker's allocation of time across tasks and the various functions of a supervisor.

One provisional observation about both the social worker data and the police data is that very few tasks tend to dominate the distributions of time during the day. For the social workers, time with clients or on paperwork accounts for a substantial fraction of the day. For the police officer, the vast majority of time is on runs (being dispatched to a particular event) or mobile patrol. These bureaucrats are invested in social activities. Why does this seem to happen?

It may be a result of some combination of artifacts. A sample selection artifact might be the reason: both social workers and police officers, by definition, spend much of their day directly interacting with particular clients by the definition of their job. Would time distributions for the more stereotypical bureaucrat, isolated behind a desk and hiding behind rules, appear similar? There are certainly such varieties of bureaucrats, but a consideration of the different agencies in the federal data leads us to think that bureaucrats typically do interact with the public.

Perhaps it is because of the crude categorizations that we use. When we refer to time spent with clients for the social workers, we are referring to a wide variety of tasks ranging from counseling to case work. A finer categorization might produce more variegated distributions, but would also make comparisons across social workers less feasible.

Conclusion

In examining the functions of the supervisor, we have explored the various roles of rules, routines, time allocation, and the brokering of trust, each of which relate in different ways to supervision. Theoretical work regarding the ambiguity of organizations features the role of task prioritization, authority relationships, and the appropriate design of the division of labor. Each of these factors, in turn, relates directly to the functions of a supervisor. Drawing (as in our previous chapters) on the data collected from a survey of North Carolina social workers, we are able to examine the nature of the connection between the trust in a bureaucracy and the allocation of tasks. Our analysis revealed several interesting patterns. Two tasks in particular dominate, time with clients and on paperwork. Given the nature of social work, this is not surprising. What may be more interesting is that subordinates' time spent with their supervisors is uniformly low.

These results hold when the data is reformulated into percentages of total time in a week devoted to various tasks. These percentages take on the form of compositional data, in that they comprise a whole. In this case the total allocation of time in a week. To evaluate the relationship between allocations of time across tasks, we draw on the Dirichlet distribution.

Organizational reliance on rules and routines results in a general pattern by which subordinates reduce the amount of time they spend with clients and spend more time on paperwork. The connection between paperwork and rule-based organizations is not so surprising. Most rules and regulations in a social work agency will involve filling out paperwork.

Trust plays a key role in determining how subordinates allocate their time across tasks. We examine the role of trust from a variety of perspectives. From our compositional analysis and our checkerboard simulations, we find the degree of trust between a supervisor and subordinate is significantly associated with a decline in paperwork and more time with clients. Other aspects of trust, such as providing protection from the outside world, is as well. Clearly, supervisors can play a critical role in reducing the need to rely on rules and routines (that is, paperwork) to address issues of organizational ambiguity.

The public's trust in government has in recent years become a significant issue. Trust profoundly affects the relationship between subordinates and supervisors. Even when taking into account the many functions of the public executive, we find trust plays a critical role in shaping how bureaucrats do their job.

Chapter 8

Leadership: Middle Managers and Supervision

THE MOST conventional view of leadership in political organizations is that leadership trickles down from the top. For example, Daniel Carpenter's *Forging Bureaucratic Autonomy*, uses the example of people such as James Wilson and Montgomery Blair (2001). Wilson helped shape the units of the federal bureaucracy in such fundamental ways that the Department of Agriculture transformed from a pork-barrel seed distribution agency to a research organization. Blair, the Civil War–era postmaster general, helped to convert a patronage laden postal service into a railway army providing free mail delivery. Indeed, most histories of public sector entrepreneurship focus on the "man on top" (and it historically has usually been a man). Whether viewed as pioneers or great reformers, entrepreneurship is typically vested at the top of the organization.

Of course, the top may not necessarily be the nominal top. Hugh Heclo's *Government of Strangers,* after all, tells more stories about the capture of the agency chief by the agency than the reverse (1977). In this regard, leadership may not be all that dispositive a force.

There is also a common presumption that middle managers are essentially powerless. Rosabeth Kanter's *Men and Women of the Corporation* describes the state of powerlessness and paralysis that managers in the middle ranks of a bureaucracy may have in influencing the organization, either by reaching upwards, or in persuading downwards (1977).

We want to press a different point: middle managers have more capacities for influence than the disciplines of political science, public administration, or economics acknowledge.

After all, nearly every supervisor is accountable to someone further up the bureaucratic hierarchy. Officers and detectives in the police force are accountable to their sergeants, those sergeants are accountable to chiefs, and so on; street-level social workers and case workers are accountable to their managers, who are accountable to supervisors, and so on up through the division directors.

One core claim of this book has been that the basic problem facing all bureaucrats—no matter what level—is the inherent ambiguities bureaucracies must manage. There are ambiguities in what we do (task ambiguities), in how we should approach them (role ambiguities), in the purposes the organization serves, the conflicts among those purposes, perhaps also the appropriateness of a matching between what we do and why we should do it.

To be sure, one of the powers of middle managers is their ability to minimize the effects of ambiguities on both their subordinates, the public, and the remainder of the organization. Consistency as a response to the demands of ambiguity is a long-known attribute of bureaucracies. But so is ethicality: appropriate flexibility is another capacity of middle managers in situations of ambiguous choice. Here we also want to emphasize that we are not arguing that ambiguity can be eliminated. Supervisors can reduce ambiguity, but they can never eradicate it. The multiple task assignment problem in particular is going to create ambiguity.

The central thesis of this book is that three particular functions of middle managers are closely linked: training, trust building, and task allocation. In a nutshell, supervisors who are able to reduce the ambiguity of a situation by clarifying the bounds of behavior put themselves under the obligation to stand up for their employees, for which they receive greater latitude in their ability to allocate tasks across subordinates. Of course, we do not mean to preclude any of the other plausible functions of supervisors, but do wish to emphasize the unique functionality of these three. In doing so, let us review the argument of the book.

The Argument

The book is organized into three parts, each pertaining to training, task allocation, and trust building. Part I outlines what training may and may not accomplish for the supervisor.

In chapter 2, we draw on several bases of survey and observational data to discuss the success of supervision as a clarification of boundaries. Chapter 2 provides us with an opportunity to examine the three surveys of the federal bureaucracy conducted in 1998, 1999, and 2000 on three dimensions: training, clarity of the boundaries, and sense of rewards within those boundaries. We also introduce the 2000 Survey of North Carolina Social Workers, which addresses components of the same problems.

Training might refer to several things: supervisory statements about the mission of the organization, explicit references to training programs, whether the subordinates believe they are equipped for the job at hand, perhaps even the extent to which the supervisor appears to be organized. Supervisors fare quite well with regard to all of these elements. In the federal survey data, the subordinates (in the aggregate) generally agree that the manager does a good job of expressing the mission of the agency, that employees receive the training they need to accomplish that mission, and that the supervisor is organized. There is a bit of slippage on whether the employees believe that the employees continue to be trained, but it is still generally positive. Perhaps the most remarkable aspect is the consensus on all dimensions in these truly enormous surveys. The patterns are similar for the North Carolina surveys: social workers in that state believe that they are receiving the training they need and that their supervisors do a good job at communicating the mission of the agency.

To be sure, there are exceptions, but keeping an eye on the main story, the exceptions are exceptional, outliers on an otherwise consistent set of beliefs.

The next question is whether the training programs accomplish what we argue that they should: establish clear boundaries about appropriate behavior. Here the evidence is overwhelming: supermajorities of the respondents see the service goals of their respective agencies as being clear. Perhaps more disquieting is their belief that feedback and the clarity of standards do not assist their performance. A lesson, perhaps, is that federal agencies could do better by making both feedback and standards more useful for the subordinates in the bureaucracies.

A more mixed message emerges from our analysis of the federal employee beliefs about their rewards on the job. Rewards might refer to pecuniary benefits such as advancements in rank or pay, reassignments to more lucrative or interesting positions, or perhaps to simply more satisfying ones. As for the general results on rewards, the respondents to the federal employee surveys generally do not believe that they are distributed by merit, and are mixed in their opinions about rewards for creativity and team effort. Unfortunately for us as analysts, it is unclear what factors bureaucrats believe are shaping the distribution. Then again, they may not have a definitive answer other than that rewards are not distributed by merit.

Asked, however, about rewards in terms of self-satisfaction on the job and for possibilities for involvement in the decisions of the agency, the respondents are much more positive. Distribution of opinions about recognition for what the employee has accomplished is far more uniform, and here, too, is an area with room for improvement in supervision. The social workers of North Carolina would generally agree here as well: accomplishment, making a difference, and gaining respect are all positive aspects of their difficult jobs.

Not surprisingly, in agencies in which the employees have more latitude in what they can accomplish, these measures are all stronger.

Employees at NASA, for example, feel not only that the supervisors lead, that the boundaries are clear, but also that they are rewarded for their achievements. Not surprisingly, too, employees across all these agencies find that their sense of being rewarded lags behind their beliefs about training and the clarity of boundaries.

Thus we conclude that one powerful, useful function of the public executive is to train by making clear what works and what does not within the organization. But let us be explicit: with the ambiguity that confronts all of these organizations, training and the clarity of boundaries does not mean that the organization has found the "right" solution, only one that all of its members can accept.

In return, we argue, supervisors have a further role to play: by setting the boundaries, the supervisor has to accept responsibility for standing up for her or his subordinates. There are many impediments and incentives for stepping away from this responsibility. Other supervisors may encroach on the actions of subordinates in other aspects of the agency: Can you just handle this, it won't take much time? What you're doing affects what happens with my people. You are working at cross-purposes with me. Stop it or else. These are familiar enough expressions by supervisors within the same or even competing agencies, politicians, and members of the media. Supervisors win the trust of their subordinates by shielding them from such encroachments.

Chapter 3 is a computational model drawing directly from the ideas of the core models of the relationship between a supervisor and subordinate,[1] but specifically endowing the supervisor with the capacity to divert resources for the purposes of cultivating pro-social preferences on the part of the subordinates. The results can be thought of in terms of what such a model indicates in the gains for the supervisor and for the subordinate. For the supervisor, such a scheme works only when the subordinates are predisposed to favor the pro-social condition and the supervisor has the means to do so. Only amenable workers are worth diverting supervisory energy. Some workers will remain essentially inert, no matter what the supervisor invests. Some workers will become increasingly counterproductive, effectively sabotaging the supervisor's efforts.[2]

For the subordinate, the story is very different. Supervisors who spend more of their resources to cultivate pro-social preferences (again, restricted to the set who are predisposed to prefer pro-social conditions) find their subordinates are increasingly happy with their conditions.

We took these results to be a reaffirmation of the debates of nearly seventy years ago, in the so-called human relations school of management. This school sought to improve on the Taylorist formulations of management as mere giving orders by recognizing that the mode and manner of command mattered as much as the command itself. The observational results from implementations of these ideas were decidedly mixed, sometimes leading to long-term improvements in productivity, other times not.

In Part II, we explore the problem of task allocation. Chapter 4 offers a game theoretical treatment of the possibility of finding a solution to the problems of task allocation. The model is somewhat at odds with the conceptions of the task allocation problem in general in that it is a cooperative rather than a noncooperative game. One could, as in the noncooperative game, think of the task allocation problem as a matter of command. The idea of the model in this chapter is to illustrate that it is possible to produce a cooperative solution—a core allocation—under which a certain distribution of perks within the bureaucracy can achieve a stable solution.[3] The important point featured by this model is that such a stable solution is attainable with a limited budget by allocating perquisites and other non-pecuniary benefits. An incentive scheme that leads to an efficient allocation of bureaucrats to tasks is attainable in the public sector.

Chapter 5 suggests that the division of tasks affects other features of subordinate performance: functional and solidary preferences.[4] Officers who were more satisfied with their contact with fellow officers also spent more time on their paperwork. Further, officers who were more in contact with fellow officers spent more time on their paperwork than other officers. There is also an interesting divide in that officers who appear to be amenable to supervision are more likely to take up paperwork, the least preferred of the tasks, than other officers. The effects here were small, but statistically significant and noticeable.

In Part III, we explore the next step in our theoretical argument is that this exchange—make clear the bounds, stand up to outsiders—is that the supervisor can gain greater latitude in the distribution of tasks.

Chapters 6 and 7 explicitly explore this trust relationship. In our surveys of the North Carolina social workers, we found an astonishingly strong relationship between "standing up" and the subordinates' trust of their immediate supervisors. Standing up to the media and other supervisors led to 60 percent or more agreement among these respondents. Standing up to other people in the government led to more than 70 percent support, and, perhaps more telling, more than 60 percent who would strongly trust their supervisors. Survey questions like these do not generally produce such skewed scales.

The most interesting, to our view, aspect of this trust relationship is that it is highly conditional. We constructed a model wherein trust in the supervisor depended upon protection, especially, but perhaps other aspects of the job. We also expected that some of the social workers would have a sense of discretion in what they could accomplish—after all, in this state there are social workers who work in very far flung areas away from direct supervision; even in those parts of the state where direct supervision is possible, discretion is as well. If the ultimate measure is the self-reports of work and the reports of how hard the other members of the agency work, then there is an interesting contingency. Subordinates who feel that they have discretion, but do not trust their supervisors, work considerably less. But subordinates who have discretion and do trust their supervisors work quite hard indeed.

The aim of this chapter is to unify the last two of these three elements, with the core idea being the resolution of the fundamental ambiguity of political organizations, especially public bureaucracies. In particular, we want to know if subordinate trust of their supervisor has noticeable effects on the amount of time they spend on tasks. Our data again come from the 2000 Survey of North Carolina Social Workers, and the results should be regarded as quite striking. Trust in the supervisor functions in much the same way as functional or solidary preferences: greater trust means more time with clients and less on paperwork. If the purpose of these organizations is to serve the clientele and not to push paper, then trust is a very practical aspect of the relationship between subordinate and supervisor.

The trust between supervisor and subordinates is the glue that holds these functions together. Trust, of course, has meant many things to many social scientists, but we have meant something specific: the subordinate's belief (founded or not in reality) that the supervisor would act on his or her behalf, to provide protection around the zone of latitude that the subordinate may perform his or her responsibilities.

Gary Miller (2004) recounts a charming story, in the Russell Sage volume edited by Roderick Kramer and Karen Cook, from *The Good Soldier Švejk and His Fortunes in the World War*, written by Jaroslav Hašek. Švejk is a peaceful beer drinker who found a way to minimally perform his duties by simply obeying his leader's orders to the letter of the officer's command, but in doing so, found ways to frustrate the officer. Švejk's behavior is nothing all that unheard of for any participant in or scholar of organizations. Oliver Williamson described behavior such as Švejk's as contingent cooperation when, of course, the officer would have preferred that Švejk be more of the consummate cooperator. For Williamson, the officer's problem would have had more to do with the uncertainties of the subordinate's jobs and the multitude of tasks that the subordinates might need to perform (1975).

For Miller, the matter is more a question of the mutual trust that subordinates and supervisors must have to arrive at an equilibrium that fares better jointly for the pair of actors than the exploitive equilibrium that benefits one or the other. "The problem is one of coordination—creating common knowledge by all relevant players that each person can expect the appropriate behaviors for [a mutually satisfactory level of subordinate performance] from all other relevant players" (2004, 123).

Integration into Agency Performance?

Our approach in this book has been explicitly behavioral and explicitly focused on the smallest workable unit: the dyadic relationship between a supervisor and her subordinate. But there is a natural and reasonable question to ask about how all of these relationships might integrate into the performance of an agency as a whole.

If one were to follow the lines of argument of the early management scholars, a critical question is about the scalar chain of command and organizational structure. Scholars such as Henri Fayol (1916/1949) and Luther Gulick (1937) were concerned with such aspects of the organization. Chester Barnard (1938/1968), whom we acknowledge with our book subtitle, rejected such notions and went so far as to say that the coercive power of management was a fiction. One of Herbert Simon's (1945) earliest contributions to this discussion was to suggest the unworkability of problems regarding chain of command and organizational structure, and to instead argue for the ambiguity of the organizational structure in the first place. An inappropriately undernoticed article by Thomas Hammond counters Simon, suggesting that there is more value to Gulick than one notices and that he was well aware of the conflicting pressures in organizational design than Simon acknowledged (1990, 143–73).[5] And in a subsequent intellectual volley, Bryan Jones points out that the most important aspects of Simon's original argument is not so much about the suboptimal nature of decision-making, but about other limits to human capacities to function in organizations, and in turn, limits to how organizations can make the best use of human choice (2001).

And so it goes. The rather high-level exchange about the nature of organizations is why we choose to work with the smallest units of study rather than aggregates, where, in our view, the mechanisms for functional performance are unexplored.

We agree that in any dyadic relationship there may be functions of the public executive that fall outside of the executive's capacities. Perhaps the individual is constrained by civil service law with regard to coercive possibilities, or the possibilities of serving as a gate-keeper over resources, or the chances of defining the mission.

That is why we contend that the three core functions we identify here—training, trust brokering, task allocation—are likely to be within reach of public executives. The world of the public bureaucracy can be ambiguous at every level, from the street-level considerations of policy implementation to instantiation of the policy. Every supervisor has the capacity, to some extent at least, to clarify the boundaries of acceptable behavior. And every supervisor, we argue, should have the capacity to stand up and defend the behavior of subordinates who operate within those boundaries.

Notes

Chapter 1

1. It should be noted that Holmström demonstrates that there is no budget-balancing incentive scheme that can effectively induce all to work and none to shirk. The implication being that a principal should turn to other mechanisms of inducement than those featuring rewards and punishments.

2. For example, one could look toward roles such as gatekeeping, exhortation, recruiting, or even direct participation in the process of work itself. Presumably, there are other roles, too, that we do not single out.

3. Note that the what happens question need not strictly be a kind of legal ambiguity—literally, is this behavior legitimate?—but surely also includes solidary ambiguity, or what will other people think of me?

Chapter 2

1. The other cases involve those reporting neutral attitudes toward the ability of the manager to communicate and a decrease in the percentage disagreeing with the statement that their supervisor is organized.

2. This is a strong point raised in our first book on the subject, *Working, Shirking, and Sabotage* (Brehm and Gates 1997).

3. As explicated in our 1997 book, solidary preferences derive from the attitudes of others, particularly through recognition.

4. The main exceptions are those strongly agreeing that they are satisfied with their job has declined 3.7 percent from 1998 to 2000. We also note that those expressing neutral opinions about job and involvement satisfaction shifted over 5 percent. But we caution against over-interpreting these rather small shifts.

5. There was a peculiar pattern of missing data among the questionnaires (item nonresponse), inducing an unacceptable and exceptionally low degrees of freedom in the multivariate analysis below. To compensate for the missing data, we apply the expectation–maximization importance sampling algorithm that Gary King and his colleagues advocate (2001). In essence, the

method imputes for missing data on the basis of the covariance patterns in the observed data, and creates several new (five, by default) data sets. The estimates we report below are averages across the multiply imputed data sets. The earlier Durham survey was conducted in 1994 and reported on in Brehm and Gates (1997). The North Carolina survey was conducted in 2000 expressly for this book and was supported by the Russell Sage Foundation.

Chapter 3

1. The terms *adverse selection* and *moral hazard* derive from the insurance industry, and were largely explicated by Kenneth Arrow in his article "The Economics of Agency" (1985). Adverse selection refers to the condition where a principal is uncertain of the agent's type, or willingness to follow the terms of the contract (for employment, for insurance). Moral hazard refers to the change in the agent's behavior as a result of receiving the contract, and is usually specified as being unobservable. In the insurance context, an adverse selection problem arises when a prospective client conceals some aspect of themselves, such as a debilitating health condition. In the same context, moral hazard results when that client, now insured, acts in ways such that he or she may need to cash in on the insurance. The approach has had widespread application across the social science.

2. This phrase raises the question of why *Zagat's* is such a successful industry: we dispute the preferences of others all the time!

3. An extensive related research on labor contracts is not covered here; the focus of such work is on the macroeconomic implications of long-term contracts, which is not immediately relevant to our work.

4. Moreover, Arrow's impossibility theorem is essentially about the problems of aggregating interests with implications for democracy and welfare economics.

5. We assume no labor market effects are operating.

6. Sabotage can be thought of as investing effort to undercut the production of some particular polity (see Brehm and Gates 1994, 1997).

7. Our definition of sabotage is somewhat more restrictive than Thorstein Veblen's (1921) definition of sabotage as a "conscious withdrawal of efficiency." Although the origination of the word (from the *sabot*, or clogs, that weavers would toss into the loom) is more clearly along the lines of efforts that undermine production, Veblen's definition would also include activities such as featherbedding and goldbricking, which do not necessarily result in negative production. Our notion of sabotage is closer to that used by Edward Lazear (1989) where workers in a team engage in activity that adversely affects the output of others.

8. The idea behind variance reduction is to reduce the noise in a computer simulation by fixing those parameters that do not yield substantive insight into the underlying model (for further explanation, see Mitriani 1982).

9. Later we elaborate more on the types of rewards available in a public sector bureaucracy limited by civil service laws. Nonetheless, an attractive assignment, a nice office, public recognition and acknowledgment, and so on can all serve as a reward in a public sector bureaucracy.

Chapter 4

1. Our game can be viewed to reflect a monopsony, such that the supervisor is the buyer paying for work by many subordinates through the allocation of perks and supervision.

2. Aanund Hylland and Richard Zeckhauser (1979) generalize the Gale and Shapely (1962) approach and apply it to the job market as well, but do not use the Shapely and Shubik approach.

3. We do not use the more generalized assignment game that Mamoru Kaneko (1982) developed.

4. Throughout this chapter, we distinguish supervisors from subordinates by designating all subordinates with a male pronoun and the supervisor with the female.

5. Work is defined as a function of effort and time, such that $w_{ij} = f(t_{ij} + q_{ij})$, where t_{ij} is the amount of time and f_{ij} is the amount of effort allocated by i toward task j (Brehm and Gates 1997, 29).

6. By ruling out ties, we need not differentiate discrete strict cores and discrete cores.

7. This result is consistent with that demonstrated in the EPA game presented in Brehm and Gates (1997), whereby supervisory time is allocated disproportionately to those subordinates most amenable to supervision. Those who tend to do what the supervisor wants them to do without supervision are ignored, as are those who are unresponsive.

Chapter 5

1. Chapter 5 in this volume ("Task Allocation in Policing") is a revised version of John Brehm, Scott Gates, and Brad Gomez, "Donut Shops, Speed Traps, and Paperwork: Supervision and the Allocation of Time to Bureaucratic Tasks," which appeared in *Politics, Policy, and Organizations: Frontiers in the Scientific Study of Bureaucracy*, edited by George A. Krause and Kenneth J. Meier.

2. This question dominates our work together and was the major theme of *Working, Shirking, and Sabotage* (Brehm and Gates 1997).

3. These hypotheses are also consistent with the EPA model, which we explicate elsewhere (Brehm and Gates 1994, 1997).

4. Note that imitation follows much more closely with the social psychological literature of a dual-path model of persuasion, in which some are persuaded by low cognition heuristics like imitation, than it follows game theoretic treatments purporting to explain persuasion (see Lupia and

McCubbins 1998). The Arthur Lupia and Matthew McCubbins explanation explicitly regards the level of attention as a prerequisite for persuasion in a mass democratic context, a highly saturated information environment. That said, imitation can also be modeled as a problem of informational cascades (Bikhchandani, Hirshleifer, and Welch 1992) or in replicator dynamics (Friedman 1991), in which imitation can be shown to be a Nash equilibrium solution.

5. The EPA model (Brehm and Gates 1994, 1997) explicitly treats supervisory time as a constrained budget, whereas the task allocation and imitative models do not. The constraint in the task allocation game is perks.

6. An example involves multiparty voting data (Katz and King 1999). In the United Kingdom, for example, the proportion of the vote can be seen to be divided across three parties, Labour, Tory, and Alliance. In turn, the vote total sums to unity.

7. The Dirichlet distribution is a multivariate continuous probability distribution.

8. Mathematically, however, there is little irony. The Dirichlet distribution is a multivariate extension of the beta distribution (Sivazlian 1981).

9. This result is even more consistent with the conclusions presented in the EPA model, which emphasizes that those subordinates who are responsive to supervision will be the ones who are supervised and that those who are not will be left alone (Brehm and Gates 1994, 1997).

10. Civil service regulations limit the ability to design contracts and remuneration schemes.

Chapter 6

1. There are two ironies here. The first is that generalized trust in government appeared to be on the rebound, as measured by these same cross-sectional surveys, the General Social Survey and the American National Election Studies being the most prominent. The second is that social capital itself has many meanings and interpretations, from Pierre Bourdieu's view that it is inherently a property of communities, not measurable at the level of individuals, through James Coleman's presentation that it is observable at the level of both individuals and communities, to Robert Putnam's conception that it inheres in communities as norms of reciprocity.

2. Formally the subgame perfect equilibrium is {Do Not Trust; Do Not Trust}.

3. Research on focal points (or why one equilibrium should be focal) has developed only recently, despite Schelling's pioneering work in the 1960s (for reviews of the literature, see Biglaiser 1994; O'Neill 1999).

4. Obviously other options are available to a social worker to induce compliance, including the ability to remove children from the home, restrain spouses from contact with their family, certify for access to state mental health programs, in addition to the more drastic option explored here whereby the social worker decides whether to pull or prolong welfare subsistence checks.

Chapter 8

1. We feature two related models, the enhanced principal-agent and imitative models (Brehm and Gates 1997).

2. These conclusions relate, and indeed we have chosen language here that relates directly, to the enhanced principal-agent (EPA) model (Brehm and Gates 1997, chapter 2).

3. This is the normal approach taken with cooperative game theory. A typical application is to look for stable sets in a legislature. The game developed in this chapter is similar in that it identifies a stable core solution to the allocation problem.

4. As developed elsewhere, functional preferences are the intrinsic rewards that come with performing a particular task—"a job well done" (Brehm and Gates 1997). Solidary norms have to do with feelings of camaraderie and the sense of being part of a team or community.

5. It is with no small irony that we note an earlier contribution by Luther Gulick attempting to create more pro-social preferences on the part of members of the U.S. military during World War I encouraging abstinence from sexual activity during the war (1918).

References

Aitchison, John. 1986. *The Statistical Analysis of Compositional Data.* New York: John Wiley & Sons.

Aitchison, John, and Shir-ming Shen. 1980. "Logistic-Normal Distributions: Some Properties and Uses." *Biometrika* 67(2): 261–72.

Alchian, Armen, and Harold Demsetz. 1972. "Production, Information Costs, and Economic Organization." *American Economic Review* 62(5): 777–95.

Allison, Graham. 1971. *The Essence of Decision.* Boston, Mass.: Little, Brown.

Arrow, Kenneth. 1985. "The Economics of Agency." In *Principals and Agents: The Structure of Business,* edited by John W. Pratt and Richard J. Zeckhauser. Boston, Mass.: Harvard Business School Press.

Ayman, Roya, Noel A. Kreicker, and Jaci Jarrett Masztal. 1994. "Defining Global Leadership in Business Environments." *Consulting Psychology Journal* 46(1): 1061–87.

Babbage, Charles. 1832. *On the Economy of Machines and Manufactures.* Philadelphia, Pa.: Carey & Lea.

Bacharach, Michael, and Michele Bernasconi. 1997. "The Variable Frame Theory of Focal Points: An Experimental Study." *Games and Economic Behavior* 19(1): 1–45.

Barnard, Chester. 1938/1968. *The Functions of the Executive.* Cambridge, Mass.: Harvard University Press.

Bass, Bernard M. 1985. *Leadership and Performance Beyond Expectations.* New York: Free Press.

Becker, Gary S., and Kevin M. Murphy. 1988. "A Theory of Rational Addiction." *Journal of Political Economy* 96(4): 675–700.

Beneveniste, Guy. 1972. *The Politics of Expertise.* Berkeley, Calif., and London: The Glendessary Press and Croom Helm.

Bergstrom, Theodore C., and Mark Bagnoli. 1993. "Courtship as a Waiting Game." *Journal of Political Economy* 101(1): 185–202.

Bianco, William T., and Robert H. Bates. 1990. "Cooperation by Design: Leadership, Structure, and Collective Dilemmas." *American Political Science Review* 84(1): 133–48.

Biglaiser, Gary. 1994. "Coordination in Games: A Survey." In *Problems of Coordination in Economic Activity,* edited by James W. Friedman. Boston, Mass.: Kluwer.

Bikhchandani, Sushil, David Hirshleifer, and Ivo Welch. 1992. "A Theory of Fads, Fashion, Custom, and Cultural Change as Informational Cascades." *Journal of Political Economy* 100(5): 992–1026.

Breaugh, James A., and Joseph P. Colihan. 1994. "Measuring Facets of Job Ambiguity: Construct Validity Evidence." *Journal of Applied Psychology* 79(2): 191–202.

Brehm, John, and Scott Gates. 1993. "Donut Shops and Speed Traps: Evaluating Models of Supervision on Police Behavior." *American Journal of Political Science* 37(2): 555–81.

———. 1994. "When Supervision Fails to Induce Compliance," *Journal of Theoretical Politics* 6(3): 323–43.

———. 1997. *Working, Shirking, and Sabotage: Bureaucratic Response to a Democratic Public.* Ann Arbor, Mich.: University of Michigan Press.

———. 1998. "A Comparison of Methods of Analysis of Time Allocation: Donut Shops, Speed Traps, and Paperwork." Paper presented at the annual meeting of the Midwest Political Science Association. Chicago, Ill., April 1998.

Brehm, John, Scott Gates, and Brad Gomez. 2003. "Donut Shops, Speed Traps, and Paperwork: Supervision and the Allocation of Time to Bureaucratic Tasks." In *Politics, Policy, and Organizations. Frontiers in the Scientific Study of the Bureaucracy,* edited by George A. Krause and Kenneth J. Meier. Ann Arbor, Mich.: University of Michigan Press.

Bycio, Peter, Rick D. Hackett, and Joyce S. Allen. 1997. "Further Assessments of Bass's (1985) Conceptualization of Transactional and Transformational Leadership." *Journal of Applied Psychology* 80(4): 468–78.

Cacioppo, John T., and Richard E. Petty. 1982. "The Need for Cognition." *Journal of Personality and Social Psychology* 42(1): 116–31.

Camerer, Colin, and Martin Weber. 1992. "Recent Developments in Modeling Preferences: Uncertainty and Ambiguity." *Journal of Risk and Uncertainty* 5(4): 325–70.

Carpenter, Daniel P. 2001. *Forging Bureaucratic Autonomy: Reputations, Networks, and Policy Innovation in Executive Agencies, 1862–1928.* Princeton, N.J.: Princeton University Press.

Cleveland, William S. 1985. *The Elements of Graphing Data.* Monterey, Calif.: Wadsworth.

Cohen, Michael D., and Robert Axelrod. 1984. "Coping With Complexity: The Adaptive Value of Changing Utility." *American Economic Review* 74(1): 30–42.

Cohen, Michael D., James G. March, and Johan P. Olsen. 1972. "A Garbage Can Model of Organizational Choice." *Administrative Science Quarterly* 17(1): 1–25.

Crawford, Vincent P., and Elsie Marie Knoer. 1981. "Job Matching with Heterogeneous Firms and Workers." *Econometrica* 49(2): 437–50.

Cropanzano, Russell, and Thomas A. Wright. 2001. "When a 'Happy' Worker is Really a 'Productive' Worker: A Review and Further Refinement of the Happy-Productive Worker Thesis." *Consulting Psychology Journal: Practice and Research* 53(3): 182–99.

Cyert, Richard M., and Morris H. DeGroot. 1975. "Adaptive Utility." In *Adaptive Economic Models,* edited by R. H. Day and T. Groves. New York: Academic Press.

Cyert, Richard M., and James G. March. 1963. *A Behavioral Theory of the Firm.* Englewood Cliffs, N.J.: Prentice-Hall.

Deci, Edward L., James P. Connell, and Richard M. Ryan. 1989. *Journal of Applied Psychology* 74(4): 580–90.

Durkheim, Émile. 1893/1997. *The Division of Labor in Society*. New York: Free Press.

Edwards, Jeffrey, and R. Van Harrison. 1993. "Job Demands and Worker Health: Three-Dimensional Reexamination of the Relationship between Person-Environment Fit and Strain." *Journal of Applied Psychology* 78(4): 628–48.

Ellsberg, Daniel. 1961. "Risk, Ambiguity, and the Savage Axioms." *Quarterly Journal of Economics* 75(4): 643–69.

Fama, Eugene F. 1980. "Agency Problems and the Theory of the Firm." *Journal of Political Economy* 88(2): 288–307.

Fayol, Henri. 1916/1949. *General and Administrative Management*, translated by C. Storrs. London: Pitman.

Finer, Herman. 1941. "Administrative Responsibility in Democratic Government." *Public Administration Review* 1(4): 335–50.

Fiorina, Morris P. 1986. "Legislator Uncertainty, Legislative Control, and the Delegation of Legislative Power." *Journal of Law, Economics, and Organization* 2(2): 33–51.

Follett, Mary Parker. 1926. "The Giving of Orders." In *Classics of Organization Theory*, edited by Jay M. Shafritz and Phillip H. Whitbeck. Oak Park, Ill.: Moore.

French, John R. P., Jr., Robert D. Caplan, and R. Van Harrison. 1982. *The Mechanisms of Job Stress and Strain*. New York: John Wiley & Sons.

Friedman, Daniel. 1991. "Evolutionary Games in Economics." *Econometrica* 59(3): 637–66.

Fuller, Jerry Bryan, and Kim Hestler. 2001. "A Closer Look at the Relationship Between Justice Perceptions and Union Participation." *Journal of Applied Psychology* 86(6): 1056–105.

Gale, David, and Lloyd S. Shapely. 1962. "College Admissions and the Stability of Marriages." *American Mathematical Monthly* 69(1): 9–15.

Gibbons, Robert. 2001. "Notes on Two Horse Races: Hobbes and Coase Meet Repeated Games." In *Trust in Society*, edited by Karen S. Cook. New York: Russell Sage Foundation.

Gouldner, Alvin W. 1954. *Patterns of Industrial Bureaucracy*. Glencoe, Ill.: The Free Press.

Gulick, Luther H. 1918. *The Stuff That Wins*. New York: The International Committee of Young Men's Christian Associations.

———. 1937. "Notes on the Theory of Organization." In *Papers on the Science of Administration*, edited by Luther Gulick and Lionel Urwick. New York: Institute of Public Administration, Columbia University.

Haller, Hans, and Vincent Crawford. 1990. "Learning How to Cooperate: Optimal Play in Repeated Coordination Games." *Econometrica* 58(3): 571–96.

Hammond, Thomas H. 1990. "In Defence of Luther Gulick's 'Notes on the Theory of Organization.' " *Public Administration* 68(Summer): 143–73.

Hardin, Russell. 2002. *Trust and Trustworthiness*. New York: Russell Sage Foundation.

Hargreaves-Heap, Shaun, and Yanis Varoufakis. 1995. *Game Theory. A Critical Introduction*. London: Routledge.

Heclo, Hugh. 1977. *Government of Strangers: Executive Policies in Washington*. Washington: Brookings Institution Press.

Holmström, Bengt. 1979. "Moral Hazard and Observability." *Bell Journal of Economics* 10(1): 74–91.

———. 1982a. "Moral Hazard in Teams." *Bell Journal of Economics* 13(2): 324–40.

———. 1982b. "Managerial Incentive Problems: A Dynamic Perspective." In *Essays in Economics and Management in Honor of Lars Wahlbeck*. Helsinki: Swedish School of Economics.

Hylland, Aanund, and Richard Zechkauser. 1979. "The Efficient Allocation of Individuals to Positions." *Journal of Political Economy* 87(2): 293–314.

Jensen, Michael C., and William H. Meckling. 1976. "Theory of the Firm: Managerial Behavior, Agency Costs and Ownership Structure." *Journal of Financial Economics* 3(4): 303–60.

Jones, Bryan D. 2001. *Politics and the Architecture of Choice: Bounded Rationality and Governance*. Chicago, Ill.: University of Chicago Press.

Kagan, Jerome. 1972. "Motives and Development." *Journal of Personality and Social Psychology* 22(1): 51–66.

Kahn, Robert, Donald M. Wolfe, Robert P. Quinn, J. Suduck Snoek, and Robert A. Rosenthal. 1964. *Organizational Stress: Studies in Role Conflict and Ambiguity*. New York: John Wiley & Sons.

Kaneko, Mamoru. 1982. "The Central Assignment Game and the Assignment Markets." *Journal of Mathematical Economics* 10(2–3): 205–32.

Kanter, Rosabeth Moss. 1977. *Men and Women of the Corporation*. New York: Basic Books.

Katz, Daniel, and Robert L. Kahn. 1978. *The Social Psychology of Organizations*. New York: John Wiley & Sons.

Katz, Jonathan N., and Gary King. 1999. "A Statistical Model of Multiparty Electoral Data." *American Political Science Review* 93(1): 15–32.

Kaufman, Herbert. 1960. *The Forest Ranger*. Baltimore, Md.: Johns Hopkins Press.

———. 1985. *Time, Chance, and Organizations*. Chatham, N.J.: Chatham House Publishing.

Kelso, Alexander S., Jr., and Vincent P. Crawford. 1982. "Job Matching, Coalition Formation, and Gross Substitutes." *Econometrica* 50(6): 1485–504.

Kiewiet, Roderick D., and Mathew D. McCubbins. 1991. *The Logic of Delegation: Congressional Parties and the Appropriations Process*. Chicago, Ill.: University of Chicago Press.

King, Gary, James Honaker, Anne Joseph, and Kenneth Scheve. 2001. "Analyzing Incomplete Political Science Data: An Alternative Algorithm for Multiple Imputation." *American Political Science Review* 95(1): 49–70.

King, Linda A., and Daniel W. King. 1990. "Role Conflict and Role Ambiguity: A Critical Assessment of Construct Validity." *Psychological Bulletin* 107(1): 48–64.

Knight, Frank H. 1921. *Risk, Uncertainty, and Profit*. Boston, Mass.: Hart, Schaffner & Marx; Houghton Mifflin Co.

Kramer, Roderick M. 1999. "Trust and Distrust in Organizations: Emerging Perspectives, Enduring Questions." *Annual Review of Psychology* 50(February): 569–98.

Kreps, David. 1990. "Corporate Culture and Economic Theory." In *Perspectives on Positive Political Economy*, edited by J. E. Alt and K. A. Shepsle. New York: Cambridge University Press.

Kreps, David, and Robert Wilson. 1982. "Reputation and Imperfect Information." *Journal of Economic Theory* 27(2): 253–79.

Kreps, David, Paul Milgrom, John Roberts, and Robert Wilson. 1982. "Rational Cooperation in the Finitely Repeated Prisoner's Dilemma." *Journal of Economic Theory* 27(2): 245–52.

Laffont, Jean-Jacques, and Jean Tirole. 1988. "The Dynamics of Incentive Contracts." *Econometrica* 56(5): 1153–75.

———. 1990. "Adverse Selection and Renegotiation in Procurement." *Review of Economic Studies* 57(4): 597–625.

Lave, Charles A., and James G. March. 1975. *An Introduction to Models in the Social Science,* New York: Harper and Row.

Lazear, Edward P. 1989. "Pay Equality and Industrial Politics." *Journal of Political Economy* 97(3): 561–80.

Lindblom, Charles. 1959. "The Science of Muddling Through." *Public Administration Review* 19(1): 79–88.

Lipsky, Michael. 1980. *Street Level Bureaucrats: Dilemmas of the Individual in Public Services.* New York: Russell Sage Foundation.

Long, Norton E. 1949. "Power and Administration." *Public Administration Review* 9(4): 257–64.

Lupia, Arthur, and Matthew D. McCubbins. 1998. *The Democratic Dilemma: Can Citizens Learn What They Need to Know?* Cambridge: Cambridge University Press.

MacLeod, Colin, and Ilan Lawrence Cohen. 1993. "Anxiety and the Interpretation of Ambiguity: A Text Comprehension Study." *Journal of Abnormal Psychology* 102(2): 238–47.

March, James G. 1978. "Bounded Rationality, Ambiguity, and the Engineering of Choice." *The Bell Journal of Economics,* 9(2): 587–608.

March, James G., and Johan P. Olsen. 1989. *Rediscovering Institutions: The Organizational Basis of Politics.* New York: Free Press.

March, James G., and Herbert Simon. 1958. *Organization.* New York: John Wiley & Sons.

Mayer, Roger C., and James H. Davis. 1999. "The Effect of the Performance Appraisal System on Trust for Management: A Field Quasi-Experiment." *Journal of Applied Psychology* 84(1): 123–36.

Mayo, Elton. 1945. *The Social Problems of an Industrial Civilization.* Cambridge, Mass.: Harvard University Press.

McCubbins, Mathew D., and Thomas Schwartz. 1984. "Congressional Oversight Overlooked: Police Patrols Versus Fire Alarms." *American Journal of Political Science* 28(1): 165–79.

McCubbins, Mathew D., Roger G. Noll, and Barry R. Weingast. 1989. "Structure and Process, Politics and Policy: Administrative Arrangements and the Political Control of Agencies." *Virginia Law Review* 75(2, Symposium on the Law and Economics of Bargaining): 431–82.

———. 1990. "Slack, Public Interest, and Structure-Induced Policy." *Journal of Law, Economics, and Organization* 6(Special Issue): 203–12.

Mehta, Judith, Chris Starmer, and Robert Sugden. 1994. "The Nature of Salience: An Experimental Investigation of Pure Coordination Games." *American Economic Review* 84(3): 658–73.

Miller, Gary L. 1992. *Managerial Dilemmas: The Political Economy of Hierarchy.* New York: Cambridge University Press.

———. 2001. "Why is Trust Necessary in Organizations? The Moral Hazard of Profit-Maximization." In *Trust in Society,* edited by Karen Cook. New York: Russell Sage Foundation.

———. 2004. "Monitoring, Rules, and the Control Paradox: Can the Good Soldier Švejk Be Trusted?" In *Trust and Distrust in Organizations,* edited by Roderick M. Kramer and Karen S. Cook. New York: Russell Sage Foundation.

Mitriani, I. 1982. *Simulation Techniques for Discrete Event Systems.* Cambridge: Cambridge University Press.

Moe, Terry M. 1984. "The New Economics of Organization." *American Journal of Political Science* 28(4): 739–77.

Niskanen, William A. 1975. "Bureaucrats and Politicians." *Journal of Law and Economics* 18(3): 617–43.

O'Neill, Barry. 1999. *Honor, Symbols, and War.* Ann Arbor, Mich.: University of Michigan Press.

Orphanides, Athanasios, and David Zervos. 1995. "Rational Addiction with Learning and Regret." *Journal of Political Economy* 103(4): 739–58.

Ostrom, Elinor, Roger B. Parks, and Gordon Whittaker. 1982. *Police Services Study, Phase II, 1977: Rochester, St. Louis, and St. Petersburg.* ICPSR Study No. 8605. Ann Arbor, Mich.: Indiana University.

Perrow, Charles. 1986. *Complex Organizations.* New York: Random House.

Putnam, Robert D. 1995. "Bowling Alone: America's Declining Social Capital." *Journal of Democracy* 6(1): 65–78.

———. 2000. *Bowling Alone: The Collapse and Revival of American Community.* New York: Simon & Schuster.

Radner, Roy. 1981. "Monitoring Cooperative Agreements in a Repeated Principal-Agent Relationship." *Econometrica* 49(5): 1127–48.

Richer, Bill. 2000. *Defending America Newsletter,* Sunday, 5 March 2000. Accessed February 14, 2008, at http://www.mail-archive.com/ctrl@listserv.aol.com/msg37274.html.

Roethlisberger, F. J., and William J. Dixon. 1939. *Management and the Worker.* Cambridge, Mass.: Harvard University Press.

Roth, Alvin E. 2003. "The Origins, History, and Design of the Resident Match." *Journal of the American Medical Association* 289(7): 909–12.

Roth, Alvin, and Marilda Sotomayor. 1990. *Two-Sided Matching: A Study in Game-Theoretic Modeling and Analysis.* Cambridge: Cambridge University Press.

Roth, Alvin, and Xiaolin Xing. 1994. "Jumping the Gun: Imperfections and Institutions Related to the Timing of Market Transactions." *American Economic Review* 84(September): 992–1044.

Rubinstein, Ariel. 1979. "Offenses That May Have Been Committed By Accident— An Optimal Policy of Redistribution," In *Applied Game Theory,* edited by Steven J. Brams, Andrew Schotter, and Gerhard Schwödiauer. Würzburg, Germany: Physica-Verlag.

Samuel, Arthur L. 1959/1963. "Some Studies in Machine Learning Using the Game of Checkers." Reprinted in *Computers and Thought,* edited by Edward A. Feigenbaum and Julian Feldman. New York: McGraw-Hill.

Sawyer, John E. 1992. "Goal and Process Clarity: Specification of Multiple Constructs of Role Ambiguity and a Structural Equation Model of Their Antecedents and Consequences." *Journal of Applied Psychology* 77(1): 130–42.

Schelling, Thomas C. 1960. *The Strategy of Conflict*. Cambridge, Mass.: Harvard University Press.

Shapley, Lloyd, and Martin Shubik. 1971. "The Assignment Game I: The Core." *International Journal of Game Theory* 1(1): 111–30.

Shubik, Martin. 1982. *Game Theory in the Social Sciences: Concepts and Solutions*. Cambridge, Mass.: MIT Press.

Simon, Herbert. 1945. *Administrative Behavior*. New York: Free Press.

Simons, H. W. 1976. *Persuasion: Understanding, Practice and Analysis*. Reading, Mass.: Addison-Wesley.

Sivazlian, Boghos D. 1981. "A Class of Multivariate Distributions." *Australian Journal of Statistics* 23(2): 251–5.

Smith, Adam. 1776/1994. *The Wealth of Nations*. New York: Random House.

Sorrentino, Richard M., and J. A. C. Short 1986. "Uncertainty Orientation, Motivation, and Cognition." In *Handbook of Motivation and Cognition*, edited by Richard M. Sorrentino and E. T. Higgins. New York: Guilford Press.

Steinbruner, John D. 1974. *The Cybernetic Theory of Decision: New Dimensions of Political Analysis*. Princeton, N.J.: Princeton University Press.

Stigler, George G., and Gary S. Becker. 1977. "De Gustibus Non Est Disputandum." *American Economic Review* 67(2): 76–90.

Taylor, Frederick W. 1911. *The Principles of Scientific Management*. New York: W. W. Norton.

Tourangeau, Roger, Lance Rips, and Ken Rasinski. 2000. *The Psychology of Survey Response*. New York: Cambridge University Press.

Veblen, Thorstein. 1921. *The Engineers and the Price System*. New York: B. W. Huebsch.

Von Neumann, John, and Oscar Morgenstern. 1944. *Theory of Games and Economic Behavior*. Princeton, N.J.: Princeton University Press.

Weber, Max. 1947. *The Theory of Social and Economic Organization*. New York: The Free Press.

Webster, Donna M., and Arie W. Kruglanski. 1994. "Individual Differences in Need for Cognitive Closure." *Journal of Personality and Social Psychology* 67(6): 1049–62.

Weick, Karl E. 1979. *The Social Psychology of Organizing*, Reading, Mass.: Addison-Wesley.

Williamson, Oliver. 1975. *Markets and Hierarchies, Analysis and Antitrust Implications: A Study of the Economics of Internal Organization*. New York: Free Press.

Wilson, James Q. 1967. "The Bureaucracy Problem." *The Public Interest* 6(Winter): 3–9.

———. 1989. *Bureaucracy: What Government Agencies Do and Why They Do It*. New York: Basic Books.

Wood, B. Dan. 1988. "Principals, Bureaucrats, and Responsiveness in Clean Air Enforcement," *American Political Science Review* 82(1): 213–34.

Index

Boldface numbers refer to figures and tables.